TOP SECRET TIPS FOR SUCCESSFUL
HUMOR IN THE WORKPLACE

Other books by Ron Berk

Professors Are from Mars®, Students Are from Snickers®

Humor as an Instructional Defibrillator

Thirteen Strategies for Measuring College Teaching

The 7 Habits of Highly Infected People

The 8th Habit: From Infection to Sick Leave

The One-Minute Meeting

Chunky Soup for the Soul

Effective Leadership: Principles of Jack Bauer

Who Moved My Lox and Cream Cheese?

The North-South-East-West Beach Diet

Tuesdays with Dr. Phil

TOP SECRET TIPS
for
SUCCESSFUL HUMOR
in the
WORKPLACE

How to Boost Productivity and Retention,
Plus 25 Other Benefits

R O N A L D   A .   B E R K

Coventry
Press

www.coventrypress.com

Coventry
Press

COPYRIGHT © 2009 BY RONALD A. BERK

Published by Coventry Press (www.coventrypress.com)

13-digit ISBN: 978-0-9823871-0-8

Library of Congress Control Number: 2009906795

Printed in the United States of America

First Edition, 2009

Special discounts are available on quantity purchases.

For Mommy

(Anne Berk)

For all that you have done and continue to do for our family

Contents

Acknowledgments

WRITING A BOOK OF THIS HEIGHT, WIDTH, WEIGHT, GIRTH, density, and hue is a piece of cake. Not really. Actually, it requires a place to work and the support of a publication team that can turn a manuscript into a polished book. The head of that team is *Judy Coughlin*, Production Manager and "Editor Par Excellence." I am indebted to her for working her magic on this book and her meticulous attention to every detail in the publication process. She deserves total credit for the quality of this volume.

This book also meant a commitment by me to writing every day and in every place until the final work was done. The places included my home office where I could work at my PC while naked, eating M & Ms, and watching Alan Shore (played by James Spader) argue a case on *Boston Legal*; my doctor's office, where I was forced to wear a surgical mask (with clothes) because of my coughing from pneumonia, while taking notes on specific tips; and the Toyota dealer, waiting (fully clothed) for the service manager to tell me my 4 Runner should be shot, while typing the parody steps on my laptop. That's commitment.

Despite the efforts of several professionals in the production of this book, there may be substantive and editorial errores or omissions. None of these people is responsible. Ultimately, there is only one person who should be held totally accountable for the mistakes in this book, and that person, of course, is Sarah Palin.

Finally, there are close friends and family who either contributed in some way to the book or were neglected because of my obsession during writing it. I am extremely grateful to close friend and humorist *Roz Trieber,* who actually field-tested the tips with students in two of her university humor courses. Her feedback and theirs were very useful. I owe my wife *Marion* an uppercase, bold-face, 16-pt. font **THANK YOU** for her patience and encouragement, and for holding me to my promise to complete this book lickety-split. I also thank my amazing daughters, *Boo Boo* (a.k.a. Marissa) and *Cori* (a.k.a. Corinne) who typed the first draft of chapter 1; my terrific son-in-law *Chris;* my most loving, cute, and fun granddaughter *Ella;* and my *Mommy* who at 90 years old is still sharp and still supports everything I produce. My family provides me with endless sources of joy, laughter, and inspiration. Without these blessings in my life, this book would be meaningless.

Foreword

"WORK ISN'T SUPPOSED TO BE FUN," A NOT-VERY-BELOVED supervisor once said to me. "That's why it's work. If it was fun, you'd be paying me to do it; not the other way around."

I didn't stay in that job for very long—and I wasn't alone. The atmosphere we work in, the corporate or organizational culture we encounter each and every day when we clock in is vitally, critically important. In fact, organizational culture is cited as one of the primary reasons employees leave a firm—and is hands down the number one reason why employees stay.

As our culture has become increasingly mobile and fluid, with work-from-home options available in almost every industry, employers have to bring more to the table than a steady paycheck and some benefits. Quality employees—the ones who can transform your business from good to great, those employees you're not afraid to let represent your company—want more from you. They want work that makes a meaningful difference in the universe, and they want to have a good time while they do it.

That's a pretty tall order. How do you create the culture that makes your employees want to get out of bed every day and rush to work? How do you transform the Monday morning mope into enthusiasm and joy? How do you do this without putting psychotropic medications in the morning coffee?

Ron Berk has the answer. In your hands, you're holding the definitive guide on injecting humor into the workplace. This is the ultimate step-by-step manual, designed to give you control over your corporate culture. With humor, laughter, and play, you can create a work environment that will attract the very best people—and coax their very best performances out of them!

Ron's approach to integrating humor into your corporate culture is the perfect synthesis of left-brain creativity with right-brain analysis and application. You'll find humor treated seriously here, with the process of infusing joy into the workplace broken down into an easy, approachable, step-by-step methodology that can be used by anyone. It's the perfect combination of strategic, insightful business thinking with a fundamental understanding of humor and what makes funny *funny*.

At the same time, you're in for an enjoyable read. Humor is one area where the proof is very much in the pudding: Ron will make you laugh. And if he doesn't . . . well. You can always blame Sarah Palin for that.

Karyn Buxman, MSN, CSP, CPAE
National Speaker's Association Hall of Fame Award
Lifetime Achievement Award,
Association for Applied & Therapeutic Humor (AATH)
President, AATH
Publisher, *Journal of Nursing Jocularity*

Introduction

_____   _____   _____
        Signature   Credit Card No.   Exp. Date

   If you fail to comply with the terms of this agreement, Andy Rooney will knock on your door and talk to you about anything. I know you don't want that to happen.

What's it like going to work in your business? Do most employees love the thought of another day at the office, or do they dread it? Do employees enjoy working? Do they have fun on their career journeys, like those guys in the Capital One commercials? Is a positive employee relations climate a priority in your business? Whatever answers you have to these questions now could change in a few months if you want to have a "fun" work environment like Southwest Airlines, Google, Starbucks, and the top-ranked The Container Store.

If humor is executed properly, according to the guidelines I provide, your corporation and your employees have everything to gain and nothing to lose. How many times are you presented with an offer like that? Huh? It's a WIN-WIN for everyone. As a shrewd businessperson, what are you thinking right now? How about: "You have to be kidding." "Where's the catch?" "What a great opportunity." "What's this going to cost me?" (*Note:* I used quotation marks just in case you think in quotes or actually said those sentences out loud.)

Further, there are buckets of research evidence at the corporate and individual levels that indicate there are more than 50 benefits to accrue from infusing humor throughout an organization. Most of those benefits are listed in chapter 1, and the rest are reported in my articles and my book, *Humor as an Instructional Defibrillator* (Stylus, 2002). Those benefits, which include boosting productivity, increasing retention, and improving recruitment, can be significant to your financial bottom line. Consider the implications for your business.

Here's the deal. If you bought this book or are thinking about it, you will get:

- ◆ A step-by-step procedure for rolling out the humor initiative to your employees
- ◆ Guidelines for setting standards for humor that is "in bounds" in the workplace and for the types of offensive humor that are out of bounds
- ◆ Forty-five secret tips revealed only to you (and anyone else who buys the book) that will furnish every person in your business with the information they need to select and perform a variety of humor forms like a professional

◆ Suggestions for applying these tips in meetings, speeches, work-shops, negotiations, customer service, and team building
◆ A BONUS chapter on how to create TV, movie, and Broadway parodies that can be used in any of the preceding applications

Obviously, this is not a joke book. There are already too many of those available at Amazon, and my two previous books furnish tons of humor material: *Professors Are from Mars*®, Students Are from Snickers® (Stylus, 2003) and *Humor as an Instructional Defibrillator* (Stylus, 2002). Although Tip 3 provides a kaleidoscope of 52 humor techniques, the tips really focus on *concrete steps, secret strategies, factors you need to know, hints, and pitfalls to avoid* that can increase your chances of humor success, regardless of what type of humor you use. They offer ideas for improving your humor and diagnosing why it bombed. The tips are simple, straightforward, and tried-and-tested suggestions to maximize your humor potential. My motto for this book is: *Get to the point.* What is the most important information you need to know to use humor in your business? But wait . . .

This book looks like a book, it feels like a book, you bought it from somebody who sells books, but it is not a traditional book. It is a whimsical romp through a playground of tips to snap your humor to attention. It is a self-help owner's manual for HR directors, managers, trainers, and all other employees who want to use humor in their workplaces. These tips come from (1) research on humor and laughter over half a century, (2) secrets and tricks of the trade of professional stand-up comedians, (3) my own hard-knocks experience during 30 years of university teaching and 4 years of elementary and secondary school teaching, and (4) my twisted mind and bizarre imagination.

This volume is written without research citations at the end of every sentence and in non-researchy language. It's for practitioners just like YOU! It doesn't matter where you are on the humor practice continuum at this point. Whether you're a newbie trying to muster up enough courage to attempt some type of humor in a meeting or a veteran on the verge of your professional comedy debut, these tips are valuable for diagnosing why your humor got whomped. You can use this collection of tips as a trouble-shooting manual. When your humor bombs, do you ever ask these questions?

- ◆ What's wrong with my material?
- ◆ Was it my delivery?
- ◆ Was my timing off?
- ◆ Why didn't they understand the humor?
- ◆ Why didn't they get the punch line?
- ◆ What's wrong with these employees?
- ◆ Why I am doing this to myself?
- ◆ Can't I just be serious and drippy like all of my colleagues?

The tips answer these basic questions and more. They address the key factors that determine whether your employees will laugh or launch projectiles at your spleen. Some of the information in the tips may raise your delivery of humor to new levels. After your humor makeover, your employees probably won't even recognize you. By the way, the tips also explain why your humor succeeds, if you care.

As noted previously, there are 45 tips in this romp. (*Digression Alert:* Remember the musketeers in Alexander Dumas' classic work: Porthos, Annette, Larry, Darryl, and Darryl? *Digression Ends.*) Consistent with the number of musketeers, all of the tips are lumped into—yup, you guessed it—five sections: (1) choosing the right stuff, (2) preparing your delivery, (3) practicing and performing your humor, (4) employee characteristics, and (5) creating a "fun" environment, plus a special bonus chapter just for romping through these tips. Every single tip can affect the success of your humor. The degree to which this happens depends on the actions you take. The test is: *Have you done everything possible to maximize the chances of your success?* Even when the answer is "Yes," you can bomb due to factors beyond your control. At least, stack the punch lines in your favor.

Setting Standards for
Appropriate Humor

Why Set Standards?

WHY DO YOU NEED TO SET STANDARDS FOR HUMOR? WHY DO you need to read this chapter before planning any type of humor activities in your business? The reason is (Are you ready? Do you want the truth? Can you handle the truth?): Humor in our culture is OUT OF CONTROL. What we see on TV, YouTube, and *Comedy Central,* and in movies, theaters, and comedy clubs is now stretching the limits of decency. Much of this material is blatantly offensive and would be inappropriate in the workplace. I'm not saying this offensive humor is not funny; it just doesn't belong in your cubicle or boardroom.

Offensive Humor in the Culture

I think some comedy writers may have lost their minds. Has Hannibal Lecter dined on their brains? Why do so many stand-up comedians and writers for commercial media seem addicted to humor that pushes the boundaries of profanity, vulgarity, and sexuality, or is just plain *out there* to offend? Rather than reflecting prevailing norms and tastes, the humor in these products of our culture seems to be lowering them. The producers have trained consumers (a.k.a. employees out on the town) to accept progressively lower standards of language and behavior. This sinking enables their work to stand out in an increasingly crowded field. Profits outweigh whatever criticism results. Falling standards, consequently, become self-fulfilling. Each new breach of the existing "standard" establishes a new, lower standard that comes to be seen as the norm, at least until the next breach. (*Note:* This is not the type of standard you want to set in your organization.)

9

One example is gross-out body humor, which is breaking box-office records. A few years ago, a series of films from Hollywood began a trend that is still deeply entrenched in the movies. It seemed to start with *There's Something About Mary* and *American Pie*. Those flicks struck a nerve because there was enough grotesque, low humor to ensure that every single viewer would be shocked by something. Keenan Ivory Wayans, director of *Scary Movie*, feels that you have to stay one step ahead, that is, take it up a notch. You can't settle for less, not in the number of laughs or in the gross factor. You have to push the envelope because the audience expects it. And push he did in *Scary Movie 2, 3,* and *4.*

Other popular movies responded to this challenge. One in particular was characterized by relentless obscenity and crude and explicit sexual innuendo. It included sex jokes involving a girl in a wheelchair, the molesting of children, an accident-prone child injured over and over again for laughs, and depictions of animal abuse and disgusting, gross-out "comedy" designed to offend everyone. Ads stated that the star of the movie ". . . doesn't cross the line . . . He stomps on it!"

Setting the Standards

Now do you see the problem? Where do you draw the line, set the standard, for humor in your business? Despite the types of humor your employees might enjoy outside work, you need to determine the boundaries for what is appropriate and inappropriate in your work environment. Those boundaries must also be communicated to your employees. If humor is being used to foster casual banter among employees and customers, to lighten up "serious" meetings, and to facilitate learning and memory in workshops, you need to lay out the rules. The process includes five critical steps:

1. ***Humor must be adopted as a core value to be taken seriously.*** It must be an integral part of the work environment.

Using humor appropriately must be viewed as a positive attribute like honor, compassion, and integrity.

2. ***Ideally, the CEO and president should believe in the value of humor.*** The tone for the workplace environment starts at the top of the organization. The leaders don't have to be funny or attempt to tell jokes if it's not their style, but they should respect and applaud those managers and employees who do. If the top leadership doesn't buy into the humor, the HR director and other managers should still make every effort to infuse humor within their spheres of influence.

3. ***All employees must accept the value of humor.*** The morale and spirit of the organization resides in the hearts of the employees. The more employees who get on board the humor train, the greater the potential for major changes that can ultimately increase productivity, trust, retention, recruitment, motivation, and creativity.

4. ***Specific guidelines for what is appropriate and inappropriate humor must be clearly communicated to everyone.*** These "rules of the game," with lots of examples, might be presented in a workshop format. There should be no doubt in the minds of employees about what forms of humor are acceptable.

5. ***The penalties for intentional violations of the standards must be articulated.*** Humor can be used inappropriately as a weapon of verbal abuse. The emotional consequences of put-downs, sarcasm, and ridicule humor can be personally devastating.

What Is Offensive Humor?

Definition

Let's first consider what is offensive. It seems that we should know it when we see or hear it. But it's not that simple. Humor that offends is based on an individual, subjective interpretation. *Any word, object, or action that violates a person's values, moral principles, or norms of behavior is offensive.* The operative word here is *violation*. A significant violation is what offends. The determination of that violation is very personal. A group of people cannot vote by majority for what is offensive or not. It's an individual reaction.

Examples

An example of violation is sexist jokes. They offend feminists because they stereotype and degrade women. Racist humor offends people who are strongly committed to the principles of human dignity. Belching and other bodily sounds in comedies such as *Shrek*, *The Nutty Professor*, and *Doctor Doolittle 2* offend many adults because such noises violate propriety; other adults and children find such behavior hilarious.

The level of attachment or commitment to principles may determine whether the humor is offensive or funny. A violation of others, such as *put-downs,* does not produce as strong an attachment as a violation of oneself. People joke more easily at the expense of others than at themselves because they are much more committed to their own dignity and comfort than that of others.

However, self-effacing or self-deprecating humor in the form of *self-downs* is not only an acceptable form, but a highly desirable one to break down barriers in the workplace. Despite the fact that the self-down represents a "violation of self," it also provides an infinite source of humor material that can be extremely effective. It also means more than put-downs because it makes a powerful statement about the self-esteem of the person using it.

Cross-Generational Values

To what extent do your values match those of your employees? The closer the match and the greater the consistency of your choice of humor with their values, the better your chances of success. The multiple generations in the workplace provide a starting point to evaluate the match. Four generations converge in one place: Veterans, Boomers, Gen Xers, and (Inter)Net Geners. They have dissimilar values and idiosyncratic styles. The diversity of demographic backgrounds complicates this process further.

Consequently, the values and moral principles of these employees are at risk of being violated. To minimize any violation that can offend your employees, I recommend a conservative standard. *You must either share or at least understand the values and principles of your employees.* Arriving at that common ground provides the path of least offensiveness. The humor you select should follow that path and be communicated to your employees.

Effects of Offensive Humor

At this point, you're probably thinking, "Why is he beginning another paragraph right here?" Because, otherwise, this section of the page would be buck naked. Say it with me: "*Humor that can potentially offend any employee is inappropriate in the workplace.*" Why? Because it can cause the following negative emotional effects in any person:

- Withdrawal
- Resentment
- Anger
- Tension
- Anxiety
- Turning off/tuning out

After you read this list, does the word *disconnect* come to mind? These emotional effects can squash an employee's motivation or spirit, which results in a loss of spunk. Once you've lost spunk, it's over. More importantly, a single offensive joke can irreparably damage relationships between employees and managers. If teamwork is part of your organization's MO (*modus operandi*, which is Latin for "your modus needs alignment"), that collaboration could be uncomfortable or impossible based on offensive remarks made to employees. Those employees may intentionally avoid the perpetrator to minimize the chance of confrontation. This is an individual issue because what is offensive to one employee may not be offensive to another. It's open to individual interpretation.

The aforementioned *negative effects of offensive humor are exactly the opposite of the positive effects of using humor in the first place.* One primary purpose of humor is to improve relationships. Nonoffensive humor can break down barriers, relax, open up, and reduce stress, tension, and anxiety to foster connections between people, especially managers, employees, and customers. It can grab and maintain the employees' attention and ability to focus or refocus on a particular point. Furthermore, offensive humor is inconsistent with some of the attributes of effective leaders, such as sensitivity, caring, understanding, compassion, and approachability.

Categories of Offensive Humor

In the humor research literature, joke types usually fit the following themes: superiority, aggression, hostility, malice, derision, cruelty, disparagement, stupidity, sex, and ethnic put-downs. Is there anything positive or nonoffensive in that list? I don't think so.

I've identified *seven major categories of offensive humor* in the context of the workplace, where humor may be presented in a variety of forms. They include many of the above themes. Those categories are (1) put-downs, (2) sarcasm, (3) ridicule, (4) profanity, (5) vulgarity, (6) sexual content and innuendo, and (7) sensitive personal experiences.

Put-Downs

This may be the most ubiquitous form of humor. Everywhere we look, from Leno to Letterman, to images of professionals on sitcoms, to colleagues, and even to our closest friends and our families, the put-down is inescapable. Check out the regular insults spewed by Dr. Gregory House (played by Hugh Laurie) at his colleagues, boss, associates, and patients on *House.* Lawyer Denny Crane (played by William Shatner) on *Boston Legal* is just as insensitive in his put-downs of racial and religious groups and people with physical disabilities.

Tendentious or disparagement humor belittles an individual or group that has been victimized, or that has suffered some misfortune or act of aggression. Sometimes it is rather harmless in the context of kidding around or teasing; at other times it can be mean, cruel, and hurtful, albeit a powerful weapon for verbal abuse. Freud believed this to be an important function of humor, allowing people to express aggressive and hostile feelings in a "socially acceptable" manner. There is even research evidence that people enjoy put-downs more when they have negative attitudes toward the victim.

Bill Cosby was recognized at the 1998 Kennedy Center Honors in Washington, D.C., which for more than 30 years has celebrated five artists each year for their "lifetime contributions to American culture through the performing arts." Only a handful of comedians has been so honored. The first person to speak on Cosby's behalf was Phylicia Rashad (a.k.a. Claire Huxtable). Her first words were: "It doesn't take a lot of intelligence to put people down. But it takes Bill's intelligence, his sensibilities, and his grace to embrace the whole world with humor and uplift it with laughter."

Although there may be a time and a place for put-down humor, such as in those over-advertised videos of Friar's Club Celebrity

Roasts emceed by the late Dean Martin and others, the work environment is definitely not the place. *Creating humor that builds employees up rather than tearing them down is not easy.* However, yielding to the temptation to tear down can produce the negative consequences described previously.

In addition to your employees, I suggest you avoid the following specific targets of put-down jokes in any conversation or speech:

- Customers and business associates, including competitors
- Popular, entertainment, or political personalities
- Groups based on race, ethnicity, culture, nationality, gender, religion, or sexual orientation
- People with certain physical characteristics (e.g., fat, thin, short, tall, blonde, pregnant, bald, or any combination of the preceding)
- People with physical disabilities or handicaps
- People with mental handicaps or illnesses

Sarcasm

A sarcastic remark is frequently just another form of the ever popular put-down. Some people often perceive sarcasm as a sign of intellectual wit or as an elite verbal art form, even when the comment is directed at them as a put-down. Sarcasm "always has an edge; it sometimes has a sting." It is usually cutting, caustic, biting, derisive, sneering, harsh, sardonic, or bitter. In sports, coaches use it to taunt, deflate, scold, ridicule, and push athletes to perform. If you're not sure of its effect, check out the sarcasm (and other put-downs) on *House, Two and a Half Men,* and *Law & Order: SVU.*

Trainers who regularly use negative sarcasm have asked me whether there is any way to justify or rationalize its use in workshops. Read my letters: NO! What makes sarcasm so dangerous is that it is spontaneous. It's highly risky, because it's difficult to control comments that come out of our mouths so quickly. If the result is negative and directed at an individual employee, the consequences can be so hurtful and damaging that an employee may not recover from the wound for a long time.

Ridicule

It doesn't get any nastier. Ridicule may be a jest that makes fun of someone sportively or good-humoredly, but usually it is intended to humiliate. It may consist of words and actions, such as scornful or contemptuous laughter. It is usually mean spirited and malicious, and may include sarcasm or other derisive, taunting, or jeering comments.

Motives for and functions of this type of insult-humor may range from the actual expression of hostility to self-deprecation to ironic reversal, where the insult is turned around and used against the attacker. For example, in the popular comedy *Meet the Parents*, the character Greg Focker (played by Ben Stiller) was ridiculed throughout the movie by several hostile members of his fiancée's family for being a male nurse and, at the end of the movie, for his real first name, Gaylord ("Gay Focker").

Comedian, composer, author, and producer Mel Brooks describes the power of ridicule in his smash Tony-award winning Broadway musical *The Producers*. (*Note:* Brooks also produced movies with the same title preceding and succeeding the show.) In an interview on *60 Minutes* with Mike Wallace (April 5, 2001), Brooks noted that the greatest form of revenge he could execute against Adolph Hitler is ridicule:

> How do you get even with him [Hitler]? There's only one way to get even. You have to bring him down with ridicule. . . . If you

can make people laugh at him [Hitler], then you're one up on him. It's been one of my lifelong jobs to make the world laugh at Adolph Hitler.

Brooks did just that in the show's signature production number, "Springtime for Hitler."

Any personal characteristic can be held up to ridicule. A foreign accent, a lisp, a stutter, an unusual gesture, and a physical disability represent common targets. For example, one of the lawyers on the popular TV series *Boston Legal*, Jerry Espenson (played by Christian Clemenson), has a condition known as Asperger's Syndrome (a form of autism). He has been ridiculed repeatedly by his colleagues and clients for his awkward and strange physical symptoms. Be sensitive to unusual physical characteristics of colleagues. Try to understand their source and resist every temptation to ridicule them.

Sexual Content and Innuendo

This topic is the core of many stand-up routines by comedians who appear on HBO and Showtime specials and on *Comedy Central*. It is also the primary vehicle for many popular TV shows, such as *Desperate Housewives, Private Practice, Nip & Tuck, Reno 911!, Boston Legal*, and *Sex and the City*, and a large proportion of R rated movies. Regardless of the gender composition of your meeting or workshop, sexual humor is out of bounds.

Profanity

You hear expletives just about everywhere. What the "&!%#" is going on? What used to be considered locker room language is now used regularly by foulmouthed cops and perpetrators (*Law &*

Order: SVU, *The Closer*, *Reno 911!*, and *The Shield*), lawyers (*Boston Legal*), doctors (*House*, *Grey's Anatomy*), and school kids (*South Park*) on TV. This coarsening of TV and our culture suggests that nothing is sacrosanct. However, despite the increasing frequency of profane language around us, its use in jokes in the workplace is inappropriate and unnecessary. It cannot be bleeped out of a conversation or speech. Whenever it occurs, its crudity debases the level of discourse and the "discourser."

Vulgarity

Creating vulgar images and sounds for laughs, especially the flatulence and toilet humor in *Blazing Saddles*, the *Nutty Professor*, the animated PG-rated *Shrek* and *Shrek 2*, and every Jim Carrey comedy, has no place in your business. Most recently, the TV cable series *Jackass* takes the prize for "Extremely Vulgar." What an honor. The parents of executive producer Trip Taylor must be so proud. (*Note:* Sarcasm is excusable when writing about types of offensive humor.)

Sensitive Personal Experiences

Years ago, Jay Leno launched a relentless joke attack night after night on former New York Yankee Darryl Strawberry's cocaine addiction. The jokes were so cruel and inappropriate that they still stand out in my mind as one example of "humor" in this category. Entertainment, political, and sports personalities are especially vulnerable to jocular barbs about divorce, abortion, sexual infidelity, cosmetic surgery, DUI arrests, alcoholism, drug addiction, HIV/AIDS, and personal tragedies. This category includes what are called "sick jokes" in the humor literature, which make fun of death, disease, dysfunction, or deformity, usually following a significant disaster or tragedy.

Individuals who engage in humor on these topics exhibit screamingly bad taste. Do the jabs at Paris Hilton, Lindsay Lohan, Britney Spears, Madonna, Alex Rodriguez, O. J. Simpson, and Michael Jackson suggest examples of this type of derisive humor by talk-show comedians? Steer clear of this category.

Communicating the Standards to Employees

Ideally, significant change within an organization starts at the top. It's desirable for either the CEO or president to roll out the humor initiative and standards. However, if more pressing issues than humor (probably everything else on the president's plate) do not permit his or her involvement, then the HR director or other manager should assume the leadership. At the beginning of the year or another appropriate time, the director or manager should convene a meeting with all employees or groups of employees. Humor should be the only topic addressed. Here is a suggested structure for the agenda:

1. "A sense of humor and humor in the workplace is greatly valued in this corporation."
2. "Recently our board of trustees or directors (or other appropriate body) voted to adopt humor as one of our core values."
3. "Research on humor in the workplace indicates several benefits for our organization. Humor can increase
   ◆ productivity
   ◆ morale

- trust
- motivation
- creativity
- retention
- recruitment

It can also

- decrease absenteeism
- create a fun work environment
- improve memory of information
- open up communication
- defuse resistance to change
- enhance relationships
- facilitate negotiations
- promote teamwork
- reduce the negative consequences of stress, tension, and anxiety

Those benefits can change our work environment."

4. "Research has also found significant benefits of using humor for you individually and relationally. Those benefits include the following:

Humor can

- increase your personal success
- increase your employability and promotional opportunities
- improve rapport between managers and employees
- enhance your negotiation skills
- improve your mental well-being
- disarm anger
- ease criticism
- improve camaraderie
- bridge cross-generational gaps
- improve your engagement in meetings, speeches, and workshops"

5. "We want to be one of the best companies to work for. We value you and what you contribute. Change will take time.

We encourage humor in your relationships with one another, in meetings, in workshops, and in all other activities.

"However, we need to set some rules or standards for appropriate types of humor, because offensive humor can hurt people and create anger rather than defuse it. Offensive humor is out of bounds. The following categories or targets of humor are inappropriate under any conditions in this organization. (*Note:* You may disagree with my list. The point is that you need to draw the line somewhere and create your own list. That's what counts.):

- put-downs of anyone
- sarcasm
- ridicule
- sexual content and innuendo
- profanity
- vulgarity
- sensitive personal issues"

6. "We will be scheduling workshops to clarify the meaning of these categories, with plenty of examples. We will also provide lots of ideas for creating positive nonoffensive humor (see Tip 3). We look forward to your active participation in this endeavor. We may not be as much fun as Southwest Airlines or Google yet, but we'll get there."

2

Tips for Choosing the Right Stuff

T IPS 1–10 FOCUS ON CHOOSING HUMOR MATERIAL THAT IS appropriate for you and your employees. The humor must fit your audience. If they do not relate to it or understand it, it will bomb. If you follow these tips, you'll avoid the most common novice pitfalls, as well as a lot of bombs with inappropriate material. You will be successful faster, rather than having to learn by trial and error and making lots of mistakes. Your employees will notice and appreciate your efforts.

TIP 1

Identify Your Humor Gifts

Few babies pop out of the womb spewing one-liners. And even in those few cases, the doctors and nurses don't laugh because the jokes are gibberish. Although we're dished out different gifts, *everyone* has the potential to be funny to varying degrees in the meeting room. That means YOU. However, let's be realistic: I'm not talking headliner stand-up at the London Palladium—at least not until next year.

Among all the forms of humor that you can present in a meeting, insert into workshop materials, or place on your Web site, there are a few forms that are best suited for you. Your assignment is to search for those forms. This is the humor version of "Where's Waldo?" What forms are most consistent with your personal style, personality, and sense of humor? You do have a sense of humor, right? If not, we may have to liposuction it out. Oh, there it is. I knew it was inside you somewhere.

Forget what you may have heard from professional comedians: "Comedy is a *special gift*—either you have it or you don't." We are not doing stand-up comedy. Stand-up is a gift, but it is only ONE form of humor. There are more than a dozen forms that you can use in your workplace.

Here's the point: Everyone has unique, God-given gifts, abilities, skills, and talents, and some of those are in the area of humor. Right now you may not know what they are, but they're there, hangin' somewhere within you. Your potential is far greater than you can see in yourself right now. Just as many of you have a unique calling to administration, training, or Homeland Security, you may also have a calling to use humor. Pursue it and embrace it.

If your purpose is to be the best possible trainer you can be, you need to optimize your special gifts for humor. Your room is the sphere of influence where you can unleash your gifts and serve your employees in ways neither of you can possibly imagine right now. Training with humor can be an adventure beyond your wildest dreams and imagination.

If you are training within your comfort zone and using only those methods to which you have become accustomed, you have settled. You may start to believe you are confined by your own limitations and, as a consequence, place constraints on what you can achieve. For some, this may be a life sentence to a training career of mind-numbing mediocrity. If you want to make a difference in your employees' lives, you may have to start with your own. You need to risk the security blanket of what you are doing to be part of something significantly bigger than yourself, far beyond your current expectations.

Your purpose in training is much greater than your fears, circumstances, and comfort. Are you ready to step out from your comfort zone and into an innovative, exciting zone, albeit a completely new ZIP code, where every workshop will be different, unpredictable, and fun?

What you will do with your employees and what you will experience together cannot be replicated outside the workshop. "Getting the notes" will never capture what you do or the impact you have. Are you willing to invest your gifts to maximize the return on your training investment? In order to optimize those gifts, you must experiment, learn, and, above all, take risks. Mastering your humor talents equips you with the confidence to master other training talents that have not been unleashed. Just how different a trainer would you be if you were to unleash your talents, knowledge, experience, emotions, and time to benefit your employees? Right now it is impossible to estimate your impact.

TIP 2

Choose Humor Material That Uses Your Gifts

Are you a stand-up comedian wannabe? Me, too. Sometimes I wish I could do stand-up like Billy Crystal, Steve Martin, or Joe Biden. But you and I both know that's not going to happen, at least for me. We need to choose forms of humor that we can handle, those that use our special gifts. Everyone has different gifts.

Your first task is to determine your humor-related gifts, such as impersonation, dialects, improvisation, joke telling, storytelling, creating parodies, writing humor, writing humorously, or physical humor. We may not know whether we have natural gifts in these areas until we experiment with them. Our gifts also vary by degree. For example, even though I can do some improvisation exercises, I will never perform at the level of Wayne Brady on the classic TV series "*Whose Line Is It Anyway?*" We can improve our skills in some of these areas by taking workshops, but our best bet is to pinpoint the types of humor that come naturally to us. It's easier to build on our strengths than to create strengths out of weaknesses, at least at first. Once your strengths are strengthened, you can tackle your weaknesses.

I have seen numerous "humor professionals" who speak to corporate and health-care audiences throughout the country. They share one common characteristic: Their unique humor styles. They're all different. They don't remind you of Robin Williams, Ellen DeGeneres, or Wolf Blitzer. Each one draws on his or her own special humor gifts.

As business men and women and trainers, it's appropriate to emulate others and use material and ideas created by them. Start with low-risk humor that can be inserted into printed materials, such as the workshop description, outline, handouts, tests, and

Web site. As you gain more confidence, test the shark-infested waters with higher-risk multiple-choice or top-10 list format jokes or cartoons. These experiences may knock your confidence level down a couple of notches, but it should pop right back up again. As your level keeps popping, your own humor style will emerge. You will carve out your humor niche with your own material and delivery style. It will be all you.

Until you take the leap and try different forms of humor, you won't know which ones fit your gifts. It's easy to guess our limitations; it's another thing to experience them. Take a few chances. The worst that can happen is that you will revert to no humor.

Eventually, you will discover your humor comfort zone (a.k.a. "humor being"), which encompasses the types of humor that *you* can create and deliver successfully. It's comfortable for you. This is not to say you can't continue to challenge yourself and stretch your limits. The zone simply contains your anchor—what you do best. By all means, keep challenging and streeeeeeetching.

TIP 3

Take Risks with a Variety of Humor Material

Those humor gifts need to come out of your closet, your garage, your pancreas, or wherever they're stored. It will require risk-taking to discover your humor talents, but, hey, you take risks in other areas of your life, such as parachuting off the roof of your house, skateboarding, bungee jumping, and appearing on a "reality TV" program. Don't even say it. My sources tell me you do things that place you at great personal risk. The humor risk pales by comparison. Here are 52 forms of humor.

Step 1: Managers and Employees, think seriously about the following low, moderate, and high risk forms of humor. There are 6 categories and 34 forms to consider:

Low Risk

1. Bulletin Board Postings
    ◆ Jokes
    ◆ Top-10 lists
    ◆ Quotes
    ◆ Cartoons/graphics
    ◆ Pictures
    ◆ Newspaper headings/ads
    ◆ Bumper stickers
    ◆ Signs
    ◆ Parodies of rules and regulations
2. Business Forms
    ◆ Travel reimbursement
    ◆ Parking regulations
    ◆ Sick leave policies
    ◆ Letters of recommendation

   3. Internal Communications
      ◆ Memos
      ◆ Newsletters
      ◆ Committee reports
      ◆ Annual reports
   4. External Communications
      ◆ Web site
      ◆ Blogs
      ◆ Ad campaign
      ◆ Videos

Moderate Risk

   5. Meetings
      ◆ Agenda (Singing, Olympic-like opening ceremonies)
      ◆ Opening
      ◆ Reports (visuals)
      ◆ Content (graphics, table, examples, family pics, pet pics)
      ◆ Minutes
      ◆ Closing (closing ceremonies)

High Risk

   6. Speeches
      ◆ Cautions and warnings on handouts
      ◆ Questions about audience
      ◆ Disclaimers
      ◆ Funding sources
      ◆ Opening anecdote, top 10, quote, lyrics
      ◆ Organization of presentation
      ◆ Skit or parody
        OR

Step 1: Trainers, think seriously about the following low, moderate, and high risk forms of humor. There are 18 forms to consider:

Low Risk

1. Humorous material on outline
2. Descriptors, cautions, and warnings on handout covers
3. Humorous problems and assignments
4. Humorous quotations and proverbs
5. Humorous material on tests
6. Humorous material on your Website

These six low risk methods involve inserting humor into print material. You can do that.

Moderate Risk

7. Humorous questions during Q & A
8. Humorous examples
9. One-shot handouts
10. Cartoons
11. Anecdotes

These five moderate risk techniques involve presenting some form of humor in the workshop.

High Risk

12. Opening jokes
13. Stand-up jokes
14. Multiple-choice items
15. Top-10 lists
16. Commercial interruptions
17. Skits/demonstrations with music
18. Game format for exercises and test reviews

Step 2: Choose one method from this list that strikes you, one that you are willing to try.

Step 3: If you're hesitant to actually present humor at this point, start with the low risk print forms. Those forms are safe. Wait to hear the employees' reaction and feedback.

Step 4: When you feel ready, use the examples of the moderate and high risk techniques from my humor books by trying them out with a few colleagues. There are loads of Top-10 lists in *Mars & Snickers* and nearly 100 multiple-choice jokes in the *Defibrillator* book.

Step 5: Based on your field test, try the humor in a meeting or a workshop. As you build more confidence that this stuff actually works, your *humor being* will emerge. Your potential to be funny or funnier is limited only by what you are willing to try. You'll just get better and better.

TIP 4

Create Original Humor Material

Leno, Letterman, O'Brien, Kimmel, and the other late night stand-up comedians and those on *Comedy Central* spew hundreds of jokes per week. Humor permeates the airwaves. Cyberspace is flooded with jokes and other types of humor material. The problem is that all these sources of humor material are available to everyone, including your employees. Remember, all of Letterman's Top-10s are posted on the show's Website. If employees have seen or heard the material, they're not going to respond the way you expect in a meeting. You don't want ersatz laughter.

When you encounter a joke or a hilarious list that can be transformed into a top 10, consider the chances that your employees will have seen it, given their gender, age, and time availability. If they are young, single, and watch *American Idol*, they have too much time on their hands. It's likely they will have seen the material in some form, often sent to them electronically by a buddy.

Jay Leno has 20 comedy writers sending him joke material 24/7. We have zero. We don't need a pool of punch-line-riddled jokes around the clock. Some of the best humor comes from real-life stories and situations rather than formal jokes. The way you describe one of your professional or personal experiences can be a hoot. Bill Cosby has done this his whole comedy career. In fact, anecdotes are low risk because they don't have to be hilarious or even have punch lines.

The anecdote is the most common form of humor among amateur comedians (like some of your employees) and women; men often prefer to tell formal jokes. Professional experiences you have had can be presented as stories related to the point you're trying to make. Some of these experiences may have been humorous. Also consider telling true humorous stories about yourself, your family (with their permission), and your friends. Employees love to hear about our personal lives, because they don't believe that some of us have any. Those stories are as effective as a joke at grabbing their attention or illustrating a point.

TIP 5

Survey Your Employees for Humor Ideas

Since you need to penetrate your employees' world to make the humor connection, you need to get inside their noggins. Obviously, current medical reimbursement rates render neurosurgery prohibitive. How about a survey? Yup, that's what I said. The most efficient, cost effective, informative, and noninvasive procedure is to survey employees on what is in their brains. This can be administered online or manually in a group. Anonymity is crucial. Here is the step-by-step method you can use in a meeting:

1. Distribute two 3 X 5 cards to each employee
2. Say: "In the upper right corner of each card, write the numbers 1 and 2 on each side of the first card and 3 and 4 on each side of the second. This is completely anonymous so don't put your name on either of the cards."
3. Say: "Are you ready? Okay. On side 1, write your 3 *favorite comedians* from TV or movies."
4. Say: "On side 2, write your 3 *favorite TV sitcoms or comedy shows*. When you're finished, pass the card to your left." Collect the cards from the ends of the rows.
5. Say: "You did so well on the first card, let's do the second."
6. Say: "Side 3, list your 3 *favorite movie comedies*."
7. Say: "Side 4, write down a *favorite joke you've seen or heard*. When you're finished, please pass your cards to the right." Collect cards from the ends of the rows.
8. Say: "I will e-mail the results of this survey to you."

This exercise requires about 10–15 minutes for distribution, completion, and collection for a meeting size of 100–150. It would be less than 10 minutes for smaller groups. Online administration takes even less time. This tiny time investment provides invaluable information.

Now what do we do with the cards? For each card, compile frequency and percentage distributions for the responses. The goal is to end up with the group's top 10 favorite comedians, sitcoms, and comedy movies, plus a pool of employee jokes.

These lists plus the jokes supply a wealth of humor material you can tap. The employees do not know what you are going to do with this material. Therein lies the element of surprise. Interestingly, the employees' picks are often consistent with several of the programs that appear in Nielsen's top-10 highest rated programs. But your top 10s are even more accurate.

The most important point to remember is that you need to enter the employees' world and to think like them to connect in meetings and workshops. *The survey provides the most up-to-date quick read on what employees see as funny.* Just how you use the results in future meetings and workshops throughout the year is limited only by your imagination.

TIP 6

Select Humor That's Funny to Your Employees

How do you know when something's funny? TV sitcoms use laugh tracks or live audiences to cue us. Those tracks provide us with a "virtual audience" with whom we can laugh, so we can burst into maniacal cackling at the right time. Puh-leeeze. You may laugh at a lot of jokes and situations that your family, friends, and colleagues may not find funny at all. What's wrong with you? So, how do you know what to use in your workplace? Is there a "litmus test" for funniness? Yup! It's your employees. If they don't laugh, the "humor" is not funny. Their response is the only one that matters.

To get into your employees' heads, use the results of the survey of comedians, TV and movie comedies, and jokes recommended in Tip 5. You need to think like them. What do they find funny? Choose material to which they can relate. Consider the generational differences in the survey results and use jokes that fit into your employees' world.

Once you've identified jokes for an upcoming speech, test them on a few colleagues who fit into your audience demographic. They won't fake their responses. In fact, sometimes they can provide valuable feedback on how to make the material funny or funnier.

TIP 7

A Third Fewer Words, Same or Better Joke!

Edit every word and gesture to the absolute minimum to maximize the punch. Extraneous material can be distracting and slow down your delivery. Eliminate unnecessary details, especially in setting up a joke. You could lose your audience at the beginning, before you get to the punch line. They could fly off your radar screen to Never-land. Scrutinize every element in your humor to determine whether it contributes to the impact you're trying to make. Professional comedians trim their one-liners and stories to bare bones. Get to the punch.

Review the lines in multiple-choice and top-10 lists and shorten them as much as possible. Prune your anecdotes to get the biggest bang for the word. Consider your bodily movements to make sure they're not redundant and that they serve to build tension or dramatize your point rather than to annoy your audience. Even pacing back and forth in front of the room while telling your story can be unnerving. STOP doing that.

TIP 8

Choose Surefire Humor Material for Your Opening

Your success in using humor in your meetings or workshops can be predicted from the humorous tone you set in the first meeting. The audience will size you up immediately and walk out at the end of the meeting thinking either: This meeting was a smash hit, and I can't wait for the next one, or what a flop—you'll have to drag me kicking and screaming to the next one. It's a Broadway opening. For better or worse, the employees are your humor critics, thinking about their reviews of your premier. Pick your best material to model in your kick-off so the audience will know what to expect in future meetings. Set the bar as high as possible with the type of humor as well.

So how do you prepare for this opening? Plan to begin your speech with a surefire top-10 list, anecdote, stand-up joke, or any other form of humor that fits your style. Prepare thoroughly to make sure you nail the opening. However, *don't use humor just at the opening and then bore your employees to death for the rest of your speech.*

Beyond these suggestions, a higher-risk opening is a *parody*, with visuals, music, videos, costumes, and/or props. One of the best parts of the parody is the blackout at the beginning (see chapter 7). It creates an atmosphere of positive tension and anticipation in the audience. Once the parody begins with the music, the slides, the props, and so on, the developing theatrical effect in the room is incredible. The content of the parody provides the laughs. This is sure to engage everyone.

When the parody is over, the audience members are on the edges of their seats waiting to see what you are going to do next. This is exactly where you want them. You can then introduce yourself, describe your standards for humor, explain offensive humor, review the agenda for the meeting, present the outline for the workshop, and so on. But what you have done is set a tone and created an image of yourself through your speech that is unlike any other director or manager. You have distinguished yourself by using humor as a systematic tool to grab your audience's attention, set a tone for your speech, and connect with them in a unique way. Consider that the opening humor or parody consumed no more than three minutes. The impact of that opening on your audience may be immeasurable.

TIP 9

"Read" Your Audience

After testing your humor material with a few colleagues, suppose your first in-meeting attempt bombs. Maybe you did everything right; maybe you didn't. So why did you get jack-o-lantern grins, but no laughs? What went wrong? There are three possible explanations:

1. The material isn't that funny to the audience.
2. Your delivery was off.
3. Your audience was too serious, anal, or not in the mood for humor.

Scrutinize your material and delivery to determine whether you can improve anything. If nothing is changed, the problem could be your audience. Get rid of 'em. Ship in another group of employees. Kidding. The group dynamics within every meeting and the managers' or employees' responsiveness to humor are different. Each group has its own personality. Group composition and size are critical. Managers and employees may also respond differently to the same joke material.

Professional comedians refer to a 50-person audience as a 50-headed monster. Although there are different people in an audience, they respond as an entity. When the exact humor material is delivered to different audiences, comedians get different reactions. That monster may turn out to be a "good crowd" or a "rough crowd." It's difficult to predict how an audience will respond.

One indicator that some comedians use to predict audience responsiveness is the audience's level of activity before the performance. If the audience is just sitting quietly, as though they received a whale-size dose of Novocaine®, they may be quiet in their response to the comedian's humor. If the audience is talkative, loud, and rambunctious, they may be very responsive. However, there is still no guarantee. Further, audiences can turn on a dime based on something you say.

In your meeting, notice everyone's mood and activity before you begin. When they are quiet, they may be preoccupied with a project they're working on, anxious about the meeting or a topic on the agenda, or exhausted from partying all night; there just may be something else occupying their minds, or they may have heavily sedated each other. This behavior may suggest you need to locate their drug dealer. Wait, that's the wrong ending to the sentence. I misplaced the ending somewhere. Huuuumm. Where could it be? Oops, there it is. Sorry for the interruption. We now resume the original sentence already in progress . . . you're not in for a positive humor experience.

Conversely, if they're feisty, talkative, energetic, and buzzing around the room, your humor may be well-received. Being sensitive to your employees' affect before a speech may determine your humor success. *"Read" your audience before jumping into your speech.* The timing for your planned jokes may not be right.

TIP 10

Give Your Humor Three Strikes Before Throwing It Out

Professional comedians recommend *trying a joke three times before throwing it out.* In other words, three different audiences can respond very differently to the same joke. *Rule of thumb*: Meeting-wise, I suggest that you use the material in at least two different meetings or venues before discarding it, unless there is total silence or the employees throw sharp objects at your liver. If you are using formats such as multiple-choice jokes, top 10s, and anecdotes, a flat response to a couple of lines may indicate the need for revision or new lines. Something may be salvaged. The diversity of employees in one meeting after another will provide a real test of the universality and funniness of your humor.

Up-close-and-personal experience: About eight years ago, my spring graduate statistics class consisted of 115 students, 90% of them women. The key factors were in my favor. I used my best tried-and-tested top-10 and multiple-choice format jokes to open every class. However, there was a less than enthusiastic response to each joke. By the sixth week, I felt I was reading the top-10 list to myself. There was virtually no response. And this was my best material. I decided that from week seven to the end of the semester I would eliminate the "opening non-joke." When students asked: "Where's the joke?" I answered: "The jokes didn't seem to be working. Hardly anyone laughed. I'm discontinuing them." This class was just very serious. I couldn't break them down. I have never had such a class before or since, where I stopped telling jokes. The class one year later than the serious one was the most responsive graduate statistics class I have ever had.

Summary

Let's review the 10 tips for choosing appropriate humor material for your employees:

1. Identify Your Humor Gifts
2. Choose Humor Material That Uses Your Gifts
3. Take Risks with a Variety of Humor Material
4. Create Original Humor Material
5. Survey Your Employees for Humor Ideas
6. Select Humor That's Funny to Your Employees
7. A Third Fewer Words, Same or Better Joke!
8. Choose Surefire Humor Material for Your Opening
9. "Read" Your Audience
10. Give Your Humor Three Strikes Before Throwing It Out

3

Tips for Preparing Your Delivery

These next 14 tips (11–24) identify critical elements for presenting humor effectively. The thought, preparation, and effort required to fine-tune your delivery will be worth the investment. Please take the time. Nothing should be left to chance. If you follow these tips, you'll save yourself a lot of disappointment, pain, and sorrow. Further, your employees will appreciate the difference.

TIP 11

Visualize Your Humor

Directors do it. Choreographers do it. Photographers do it. Hunters do it. Dick Cheney did it. You need to do it. Even I'm thinking about doing it. "Yiiikes! What is *it?*" Visualize the image you want to project. Create an image in your mind of what you want your audience to see. View your humor image through your employees' eyeballs. Consider the following scenarios:

1. *You alone are telling a joke or anecdote*—What gestures and physical movements can you visualize that can dramatize your humor to increase its impact?
2. *You alone with props and/or music*—What size and types of props will create the greatest impact? How should they be held? How will the music be received? What emotions do you want to elicit?
3. *You with another manager or employee*—Since you two are the audiovisual, what image do you want to convey? What clothes, props, dialogue, movements, and/or music are needed to produce the desired effect?
4. *Entrance of employees to begin a demonstration*—As employees walk, hop, jog, dance, etc., to the front of the room, what effect do you want to project? How and when do you prep the employees for that effect? What clothes, props, and/or music do you need?
5. *One or two groups of employees in a demonstration*—What image should these employees present to their colleagues or management? What clothes, props, dialogues, movements, and/or music will bring the image to life? How much preparation is needed to make this happen? Do the employees have to rehearse?

All of these scenarios are planned in your mind. The humor becomes very high risk unless you visualize the effects to estimate their impact on your audience. You can't simply throw together the preceding scenarios and then hope for the best. Either plan and execute them properly or don't try them at all.

TIP 12

Slow Down to Deliver Your Humor

Slowww dowwwn, for heaven's sake. Deliver your humor at a slower pace than you normally use for speaking. Humor requires mental processing. It's a cognitive game like problem solving. In fact, the actual cognitive processing of a joke in the left hemisphere of your brain is identical to that in problem solving. The issue is that everyone processes information, including jokes, at different rates. Whizzing through a joke or any form of humor makes no sense. If it's funny material, you want to milk it for all the laughs you can get. Use the timing in your delivery to the fullest. Savor the laughs. They are the pay-off at the end of your humor.

Another reason to deliberately control the speed (and enunciation) in your delivery is to allow employees and customers who are not native English speakers the time to translate the humor in their minds. Consider the ethnic mix in the increasingly diverse workplace. For individuals for whom English is their second language, extra time may be needed to translate into their native language. Because English language proficiency varies considerably from person to person, this may not be a concern once you've gauged your customers' proficiency levels.

Be sensitive to this problem when using humor in speeches and training materials in your own work environment as well as at national and international conferences. Just slow down. Your audiences will appreciate it and, more often than not, "get the joke."

TIP 13

Enunciate Every Syllable

Stand-up comedians (as well as professional speakers and actors) have to speak clearly to allow us to process their jokes and laugh. It is frustrating to listen to comedians who speak very fast or garble their syllables. It is the same with your audience. Employees in your audience should not have to strain their hearing to understand what you are saying, especially when it's supposed to be funny. You can't present humor in the same style as a casual conversation. You must *perform* it deliberately and forcefully. Don't slur words— enunciate with precision.

Enunciation is especially critical for non-native English speakers, who must first understand the English words and then process the humor. Their level of English language proficiency will be a factor, but your clear delivery of every word will make it so much easier for them to get the joke.

With all the preparation required to deliver humor in a formal meeting or workshop, you don't want to waste that effort because you didn't pronounce your words clearly and deliberately or because you blew the punch line. Take nothing for granted in delivering humor. Precision in the language you use is critical to the success of your humor.

TIP 14

Don't Laugh at Your Own Humor

After practicing your humor a quadrillion times, this shouldn't be a problem. You will no longer find the jokes funny. But that's beside the point. Why shouldn't you laugh along with your employees? Here are a few reasons to consider:

- Professional comedians keep a straight face.
- It would break your "character" (you are performing when you tell jokes).
- Leave the laughing to your employees.
- What if you laugh and the employees don't?
- Your humor will be more effective.

There are a couple of exceptions to this rule: (1) a spontaneous remark that's funny, and (2) an exchange between you and one of your employees that produces laughs. In both cases, you are being *you*, stepping out of your joke-telling character and responding naturally to something. It is okay to laugh "in the moment" along with your audience because you're being entertained as part of your speech and employee participation. You're all experiencing something special together.

TIP 15

Don't Set Up Your Humor for Failure

DO NOT, I repeat, DO NOT preface any joke, anecdote, cartoon, or other form of humor with the following:

- "This is my favorite *(story).*"
- "*(My daughter)* told me this *(joke).*"
- "I love this *(cartoon).*"

This is a prescription for disaster. Just tell the joke. Let your audience be the judge. The joke should succeed or fail on its own merits. It's either funny or it isn't, assuming your delivery was perfect. Don't attempt to bias your audience in your favor before you tell the joke. If it bombs, then both you and your employees feel bad. They're embarrassed for you.

TIP 16

When You Bomb, Keep Moving

Regardless of what type of humor you deliver, when your room sounds like the morgue on *CSI*, KEEP MOVING. Don't stop. A quick getaway is best. Don't try to explain the joke. If you are doing a series of jokes, multiple-choice lines, or a top-10 list and there is no laughter after a line, don't pause, don't blink. Just move rapidly to the next line with as deliberate and forceful a delivery as the line that croaked. No matter how disappointed you feel at the moment, don't let it show. Act. The next line may produce an explosion of laughter. The audience will remember the laugh lines, not the bombs.

Top professional stand-up comedians typically keep moving after a joke bombs. However, sometimes they will use the bomb as an opportunity for humor with a follow-up look or punch line to save face. It's usually self-deprecating, because the audience knows you're in trouble. This lifeline is called a "Silence Saver." It may be used once or twice, but no more than three times during a single presentation. Examples you could use are the following:

- ◆ "Have I said something to upset you?"
- ◆ "I'll wait."
- ◆ "I feel like I'm rehearsing."
- ◆ "This was hysterical yesterday."
- ◆ "My daughter told me this one was dumb."

These lines can bail you out of an embarrassing situation. But you have to remember these silence savers. Occasionally, you might think of one on the spot. After the "saver," make sure you get back on track. You're also not doing a stand-up routine in every meeting.

I recommend concentrating on the positive delivery of your humor, rather than how to recover from the negative results. If you think of a silence saver at the time, use it. Otherwise, stay focused and keep moving.

TIP 17

Don't Step on Your Laughs

In the normal course of conversation, if someone laughs at something you say, the conversation typically stops, then resumes when the laughter is over. Otherwise, the laughter could drown out the conversation and our buddies would ask: "Would you repeat what you said? I couldn't hear because this big gas-bag was laughing so loudly." This same scenario can occur when you are formally telling jokes to your employees.

After you deliver the punch line, stop for a moment before continuing, to allow time for laughter. If there is little or none, keep moving. If you don't stop and your employees laugh, they will miss your next line. You just stepped on your audience's laughs. As you deliver your humor, listen very carefully to your employees' responses. Go with *their* flow.

Determining the exact time to stop for laughs and when to continue is most critical when you are presenting one punch line after another, as in a multiple-choice format joke, top-10 list, or multi-panel cartoon. As you read each "one-liner," pause to listen for laughter. If there is some, *wait until the laughter has died down almost completely.* Then read the next line. You want your audience to clearly hear and see each punch. That will maximize your chances of laughter after each line.

Very often you will feel that you are presenting the list at the pace of the audience's responses. That's as it should be. As you proceed through a top 10, your timing will establish a rhythm with your employees' laughter. The more you practice, the better your timing. Although you have 10 chances for laughter, not all lines will work. When there are no laughs, your tempo will speed up a bit; when there are laughs, you will slow down.

TIP 18

Field Test Your Humor

No professional comedian, speaker, or actor in a Neil Simon play walks onto the stage to perform material he or she has just seen for the first time. At minimum, the humor may be tested with friends, relatives, or a group of humor writers. At maximum, it is field tested in comedy clubs, rehearsals, previews, or with small audiences (a.k.a. the comedian's version of focus groups).

Since you are the humor writer and performer, the easiest and most accessible "focus group" is a few colleagues who will laugh at almost anything and tell you the truth. Try the material on one colleague at a time so you can make appropriate changes based on his or her feedback. If these colleagues don't laugh, then your employee audience probably won't. Your "test" colleagues may also suggest changes.

For workshops, nab some employees from previous workshops to get their reactions to the material. The more feedback you can obtain before the workshop, the greater your chances of success with the new group. If these employees don't laugh, your material just isn't funny. Only their responses count.

TIP 19

Use Your Voice as a Musical Instrument, but Not Bagpipes!

You have an amazing instrument behind your lips. Not your gums! Of course, it's your vocal cords somewhere down your throat. Your cords were never designed to produce a monotone lecture that induces a coma in meetings. Yet, somehow, some managers (and you know who they are) have managed to cord their employees to sleep.

When you deliver humor, vary your volume, tone, pitch, timbre, pace, and inflection. You need a microphone, preferably a lapel mic. Otherwise, your audience may not be able to clearly hear or discern the range of sounds. Consider the possibilities as you read a top 10 or tell an anecdote. Your voice can create drama by itself just by modulating the volume from a whisper to a blast. When you pause before a punch line, prepare to deliver the punch forcefully and loudly. When you lower your voice, the audience must make an extra effort to hear you. That heightens their level of attention.

When you practice the humor material, intentionally vary your delivery. To hear the effect, record it. That's what the employees will hear. If it doesn't have the impact you want, change it. Then try it out on a few colleagues. They'll tell you whether you're ready.

TIP 20

Follow Your Gut Reaction to an Ad Lib

As you're listening to a speaker, you have a "Eureka!" moment. A spontaneous comment, also called an ad lib, or a top-10 list pops into your mind that you really want to read. The problem is: Your gut, instinct, intuition, or psychic hotline caller is telling you that it may be inappropriate, too risqué, or potentially offensive to your employees. DON'T DO IT. *Follow your gut.*

An ad lib is particularly dangerous. There's a funny thought that races through your brain, and you have to make an instantaneous decision: "Should I say it or not?" When in doubt, DON'T. Similarly, you may create or find new material that you have no opportunity to field test with colleagues. The temptation is there. You think the list or joke is hilarious. But there's that little voice whispering to you: "You idiot, don't even think about it."

This tip also applies to the risk-taking situation where you are not sure the material will be successful. You're hesitant to try it and little gut-man-psychic-voice is saying: "Don't do it." My suggestion is: *Follow gut-man or gut-woman.* Don't do it.

Every time I followed these mysterious voices telling me what to do, I was successful. They were the correct decisions. The few times I didn't listen resulted in disaster. It's best to err on the side of caution when you're not sure, and definitely take your meds if you're hearing voices. A few milligrams of Clozaril® can provide an ounce of prevention. Kidding.

TIP 21

Recruit Employees to Deliver the Humor

Employees get a real kick out of an activity where their buddies are showcased in front of the audience. There is a built-in identity and connection. Instead of you reading the top 10, use the David Letterman technique of picking 10 people to read the list. Here are the steps:

1. Prepare an appropriate list, such as "Top 10 Complaints Employees Have About . . . ," "Top 10 Ways You Can Become Unpopular in this Business," or "Top 10 Tips on What Not to Say at Your Appraisal Review."
2. Make 10 paper copies and a PowerPoint® transparency.
3. Circle one number on each paper copy.
4. Before the meeting or workshop, pick 10 employees scattered throughout the room who can speak loudly and clearly.
5. Say to each employee: "When I cue you by saying the number circled on your sheet, stand up and read the line clearly and loudly." One employee might respond: "This is so lame. I'm going to bomb." Yeah, maybe, but that's okay. You'll live.
6. When you're ready to read the list, make sure your employee plants are ready. A couple of times when I was speaking, one of the employees had snuck out of the room to make a phone call or go to the rest room. I had to wait for her return before I could start.
7. Click title of PowerPoint® slide. Introduce the top 10. After you read each number, reveal the line as the employee is reading it. This visual allows the audience to see the line in

case the employee doesn't read the words loudly enough. Using both visual and auditory senses also increases the impact of the top 10.

Aside from the funniness of the top 10, the audience also laughs as each employee pops up and down (like a Jack or Jackie-in-the Box) at different locations in the room. The surprise of not knowing who will pop up next produces additional humor. When employees are part of the humor, your chances of success can greatly increase. Give it a crack.

TIP 22

Use a Microphone, Better Yet, a Lapel Mic

Entertainers always use microphones. Comedians and singers, in particular, walk onto stage holding a mic. This is an image that's deeply etched in our minds. Will your employees have that same expectation when you make your entrance? Probably not!

So, now you're supposed to entertain. The mic amplifies your voice so that it commands attention. You're louder than everyone else in the room, thanks to the miracle of technology. This can give the impression of enhanced credibility and authority. So far, so good, but you haven't said a word yet.

When professional comedians have performed the same routine with and without a mic, the difference was significant. Comedians report that when they used a mic, the audience laughs were much louder, more frequent, and more enthusiastic. Go figure. Can holding a 10-inch steel pipe make that big a difference in laughs? At least, it provides the illusion of entertainment and credibility.

Clearly, the *handheld mic* is the "industry standard" for professional stand-up comedians. They prefer either the cordless variety or corded mic on a stand, but NOT the *lapel mic*. The latter clips to your shirt, tie, or even your lapel with a wire attached to a small transmitter pack you hook on your belt. There is also a *wired ear mic* (also called the Madonna mic, which, of course, is named after the pop super-star Britney Spears) which fits around your nose, oops, I mean ear with a wire attached to a transmitter (*Gender Alert:* Ladies, I recommend wearing a suit, pant suit, or jacket so you have a place to clip the mic *and* the transmitter. Even with the wired ear mic you need a place to stick the transmitter. The latter can be very tricky with a dress or swimsuit. *End of Alert.*)

Handheld means handheld mic, not lapel held. The "pro look" is associated with the handheld mic. It is preferred because, when the punch line to a joke is delivered, the mic can be moved closer to your mouth as you say the punch louder. You can raise your voice with a lapel mic, but it's not the same.

How does this relate to your speech? First, boardrooms and other larger rooms that can accommodate 10–50 people usually do not have any type of mic or sound system available. That leaves you few options. You can try holding a real or toy mic (not connected to a sound system) or a piece of steel pipe to see if it makes a difference. That might get a laugh by itself. Second, larger rooms, such as auditoriums, theaters, or lecture halls, usually come equipped with a mic stuck in the lectern or a lapel mic. Use the lapel or wired ear mic. It will allow you to move around freely unless it's tied to an umbilical cord.

My recommendation is (Are you sitting down? This is exciting, isn't it?): *Use a lapel or wired ear mic in any size room where it is available*! I have 5 reasons that are totally different from the "pro look": (1) a mic allows your audience to hear every word clearly, no matter where you are in the room, (2) it permits you to modulate the volume, tone, and inflection in your voice in an anecdote and be heard perfectly, (3) it allows you to walk out into your audience to be closer to them, (4) it gives you freedom to turn in any direction and use your body language and still be heard, and (5) it frees both hands to put on a costume, use props, manipulate the Powerpoint® remote, or gesticulate. Whatta ya think? Give it a try.

TIP 23

Prepare Employees to Participate in Demonstrations

If any employees are needed for a parody or demonstration, ask them well in advance. If they consent, give them two-week, one-week, two-day, and one-day reminders with the approximate time. The day before the demonstration, I usually e-mail the 15-minute window when I expect to begin the skit. If they need to wear something special or walk in with props, make sure they remember that as well. Also, don't forget to tell them the room number. If the skit requires rehearsals, plan those a few weeks in advance so there is adequate time to prepare and no one feels rushed.

The skill necessary to participate in demonstrations is ambulation or, at least, mobility. If the employees can walk (or roll in a wheelchair) to the front of the room and stand (or sit), they qualify. There is no dialogue to memorize. They serve as visual images of concepts, processes, or live research data. They are walking (or sitting) metaphors. You will direct their movements to illustrate the point.

When certain clothing is required, such as hooded sweatshirts for *Rocky* or white gloves for *Chicago*, tell employees a week before the scheduled demonstration. From the first demonstration, employees should know what to expect. Invoke the "safe environment rule" so they know you will never embarrass or humiliate them. If you ever violate that rule, the demonstrations are over. The trust is blown. No one would consider participating.

For different meetings or workshops, ask different employees to participate. This maintains the critical humor ingredient of surprise. The employees never know when it's coming or who is in it. It also spreads around the participation so you can involve a lot of employees. Acting in a demonstration should be a badge of honor. At the end of the year, consider awarding Oscars to the best or most memorable performances.

Meet with the employees individually or in a small group just before the speech. Tell them exactly what you want them to do:

- where to sit
- the cue to stand up and come down to the front
- what aisle to enter (so everyone doesn't crash into one another)
- where to stand when they get to the front
- what will happen when they're in front of the room
- the music they will hear
- walk, jog, dance
- arm movements or gestures
- what to do with props

Once you give these instructions, the employees will have no fear or hesitancy about participating. They know everything that will happen. They trust you completely. Make sure they don't say a word about any of the instructions to their buddies. It's all top secret, high security. Remember, the security level is chartreuse.

TIP 24

Test All Technical and Audiovisual Equipment

I know you've already prepared everything for your speech. The music and videos in your PowerPoint® slides are ready to go. And Barry White is ready to sing: "You're my first, my last, my evvvvery-thing." But still, before you leave your office for the meeting, just for me, please test one last time. On occasion, I have forgotten to reset my slides to the beginning, turn off my security and virus scanner, reset the volume level on my PC, and check the battery level of my lapel mic.

Hopefully, you have at least 15 minutes to set up before your speech begins. Use your own laptop. Connect the electrical cord, then plug the LCD cable into the VGA port and audio cable into the audio output port. Check sound levels for the music and lapel mic. If you have videos with blackouts, prepare a lighting script of the slides a technician can follow during your speech. If you have several music and video slides embedded in your PowerPoint® speech, I recommend having a separate rehearsal with a technician to make sure every slide changes smoothly with appropriate volume levels and blackouts.

Set the volume between 3–6 db so you don't blow out your employees' eardrums or brains. They're going to need their multiple intelligences. *Never use your real humor material to test equipment.* Insert test slides at the beginning of your PowerPoint® so you don't give away any of the goodies.

Always keep back-ups. I have AA and AAA batteries with me at all times, especially for the mic and remote changer. Always check the battery level of the mic. I've had the battery in the mic die just as I tested it. I replaced it on the spot rather than during the top 10 or parody, which would have blown the timing of the delivery.

Finally, if you're using a blackout to open any skit or videos, check which light switches need to be hit. It's best to ask a technician how the lights are configured. Also close window shades, blinds, or drapes and cover glass panes in doors where the light shines in. You want a total blackout of the room for the maximum theatrical effect. Sometimes light will spill in and dilute that effect and the color of the slides. Also, don't forget one or two small flashlights so you can see what you're doing once the lights go out. While your crashing into tables may sound funny, you should also try to execute the humor you planned.

Summary

Let's review the 14 tips for delivering humor in the workplace:

11. Visualize Your Humor
12. Slow Down to Deliver Your Humor
13. Enunciate Every Syllable
14. Don't Laugh at Your Own Humor
15. Don't Set Up Your Humor for Failure
16. When You Bomb, Keep Moving
17. Don't Step on Your Laughs
18. Field Test Your Humor
19. Use Your Voice as a Musical Instrument, but Not Bagpipes!
20. Follow Your Gut Reaction to an Ad Lib
21. Recruit Employees to Deliver the Humor
22. Use a Microphone, Better Yet, a Lapel Mic
23. Prepare Employees to Participate in Demonstrations
24. Test All Technical and Audiovisual Equipment

4

Tips for Practicing and Performing Humor

THESE NEXT SEVEN TIPS (25–31) PROVIDE A GUIDE TO PER-
forming humor material at a professional level. There isn't a lot of
wiggle room for errors in presenting humor. You need to consider
whether you want to do it right or not at all. If you follow these
tips, you'll avoid the most common preparation mistakes by practicing your performance so it will have professional polish. You will
be successful faster, instead of learning these elements by trial and
error. The response by your employee audiences should provide
the reinforcement for your efforts.

Mentally Practice Your Humor

You are the writer, director, and choreographer of your material. Think about every word, gesture, facial expression, visual image, and sound you want to transmit. Have you chosen the most appropriate and succinct wording? Are the gestures exaggerated enough? Are they dramatic? How will your facial expressions be received? Will you make eye contact? What will the overall visual image look like? How will the music affect the mood? Will it be loud enough? Do the sound effects add or detract from the overall effect?

Answer every question that applies and make adjustments. Run these images and sounds through your mind multiple times until you've reached resolve on the final product. Then practice it mentally until you know exactly how you're going to perform your material. Think about every phase of your delivery. Consider the timing and body image from the punch. Now you're ready to physically rehearse the whole package.

TIP 26

Physically Practice Your Humor

Am I being redundant? Perhaps. The late Broadway director and choreographer Bob Fosse was notorious for the demands he placed on the cast members in his shows, such as *Damn Yankees*, *Pajama Game*, *Chicago*, *Liza with a "Z," Dancin'*, and *Cabaret*. It was not unusual for him to rehearse a single dance routine 100 times or more. During a rehearsal for *How to Succeed in Business without Really Trying*, a male dancer in the chorus complained, "We've already done this 50 times." Fosse, who was all the way across the stage, puffing on his cigarette, heard the comment, turned his head, looked directly at the dancer, and said, "Thank you very much, you can pick up a plane ticket home in my office," which meant: "You're Fired!"

Is it possible to practice too much? I don't think so. Presenting humor is performing. Consider the time you have already spent preparing the humor, demonstration, music, props, or other elements. Although we're not professional comedians, delivery of humor or performing with any of this material requires precision. You can't wing it. (Robin Williams could, but not us.) Practice it in your mind, then practice it in front of a mirror to see every expression and movement. Listen to your every pause, inflection, and tone. Timing is critical. Practice as many times as possible in the time you have. Only through practice will you be able to keep polishing your delivery until you're ready for "Showtime." *Your humor should appear smooth and effortless to your employees.*

No matter how many times I practice a stand-up joke, top-10 list, or skit with music and props, it is different every time. When I finally perform it in front of an audience, it's different from my practice sessions. And every performance is different. I am regularly humbled by the mistakes I make or something unexpected that occurs. For example, I may stumble over a word, the remote may skip over a one-liner, the music may not play with the slide, or the lapel mic battery may die. Even practice won't make it perfect. We depend on the technology and ourselves, both of which are fallible.

The primary value of practice is to know you've done everything within your power to nail that joke or skit. Those factors beyond your control that can ruin your effort will occur anyway. They're simply not within your purview. Practicing your delivery, gestures, music, and use of props is. Do it and you won't regret it. You'll have many more hits than misses.

TIP 27

Practice the Timing of Your Verbal Humor

Timing in the comedy world often focuses on the classic "pause" before delivering the punch line. With the variety of humor forms I have suggested for use in the workplace, timing goes far beyond the single punch. It involves the pacing in your delivery. Presenting verbal humor, such as one-liners, anecdotes, multiple-choice jokes, top-10 lists, and cartoons with captions or bubbles, requires deliberate pacing or rhythm. The delivery should be strong and slower than your normal speech. Your employees are not just listening; they're processing. Verbal humor involves the same cognitive functioning as problem solving. And your employees process at different speeds.

One-liner-based humor has to be timed with your employees' responses. For example, multiple-choice (4–5 one-liners) and top-10 formats can only be read at the pace of the response to each one-liner. Although you pause before each punch, you don't want to step on the laughs by moving too fast through the list. Just listen carefully to your audience. As the laughter drops off, proceed to the next line. This timing comes with practice.

TIP 28

Practice the Timing of Your Music

Music can be used as a punch line to trigger laughter, introduce a topic or skit, accompany a demonstration, or conclude a speech. There are more than a dozen techniques for using music in speeches. The timing of the music is crucial to any parody and the humor you've written. There are a few factors to consider:

Equipment: CD player, iPod or MP3 player should be inserted into the speaker dock system, or music inserted into PowerPoint® slides with LCD and VGA and audio cables.

Location: The equipment must be organized and easily accessible on a table.

Timing: When you click the slide, the music clip must play on cue and at the correct volume. Make sure the volume has been set previously. It's inconvenient and distracting to make adjustments during a demonstration, unless a tech person is available to handle that. If you press the wrong slide or track, you're done. The reliability of your equipment and the timing of the music are critical to executing the demonstration. So that the melody or lyrics will be immediately recognizable to the audience, make sure you cut the extract to produce the desired effect. The cut should begin with the lyrics you want. All of these elements involve preparation and practice.

TIP 29

Practice the Timing for Putting on Costumes

If you perform parodies or demonstrations, even the simplest costume or accessory needs to be donned with perfect timing. I don't recommend ornate or complex costumes, such as those in *Cats*, the Egyptian robes in *Aida*, or the vertebrae-breaking, cartilage-tearing headwear in *The Lion King*. You must be able to put on the costume quickly, and it must be easily accessible, but hidden from view of your audience. Even a hideous orb pendant from the Joan Rivers collection hawked late at night on QVC would be appropriate. Consider the following:

Examples: hat, glasses, wig, cape, tool belt, scarf, smoking jacket, poncho, sweater, sneakers

Location: Hide on the table in a canvas bag, under the table, or on the side of the table in a backpack

Timing: Plan exactly how and when you are going to put on the costume and take it off. For example, small hats, glasses, or a scarf can just be pulled out of a bag. When I am presenting a more elaborate production, I might begin with a blackout. Then I drop below the table, put on the wig, cape, etc., press the button for the music, then rise slowly as the lights are turned on. Each movement must be deliberate and timed with precision. If you end up fumbling around in the dark looking for the hat or press the wrong button on the PowerPoint® remote, the parody is over. You've blown it. It's very hard to recover. Rehearse the procedure with the costume several times to prevent any possible glitches from occurring during your performance.

TIP 30

Practice the Timing for Handling Props

The steps for handling props in a speech are very similar to those used with a costume. The major difference is you don't wear props. Your hands must be free to handle them. Keep in mind, the props I'm suggesting you use in parodies are not on the scale of the gargantuan, roving chandelier in *The Phantom of the Opera* or the helicopter in *Miss Saigon*. No elaborate light fixtures or whirlybirds. Think a bit smaller. Here are the key elements, with examples:

Examples: swords, light sabers, sparklers, cigar, flashlights, headlights, crime scene tape, knives, inflated aliens, sharks, tools, umbrella, flags

Location: Depending on size, a prop can be hidden in a bag on or under a table

Timing: As noted above, you need one or both hands to grab the prop(s) quickly, hold it for the duration of the skit, and then put it someplace out of the way. Since the props may be used any time during the speech, you need to plan these steps. If you're holding a mic, remote control, laser pointer, or notes, you can't hold props. A lapel or wired ear mic leaves your hands free. The timing for grabbing a prop based on a music cue, for lighting it or turning it on in a blackout, for moving it, turning it off, and putting it away must be practiced several times. Rehearse, rehearse, rehearse.

TIP 31

Practice the Timing for Demonstrations

A demonstration may involve all of the technical equipment described in the preceding tips plus one or more humans. Now the plot thickens. Employee participants must know their cues. Again, it's all about timing. You must orchestrate the entire production, which can include:

- handling props
- turning on the music
- turning off room lights
- cuing the employees

All of this must be coordinated by you. By now you're probably thinking: "The timing in delivering the punch line to a joke seems a lot easier than trying to remember all of this stuff." In print, it can appear complicated. However, if I demonstrated the process for you once or twice, you would pick it up easily. Like anything else, it just takes practice.

Summary

Let's review the seven tips for practicing and performing humor in the workplace:

25. Mentally Practice Your Humor
26. Physically Practice Your Humor
27. Practice the Timing of Your Verbal Humor
28. Practice the Timing of Your Music
29. Practice the Timing for Putting on Costumes
30. Practice the Timing for Handling Props
31. Practice the Timing for Demonstrations

5

Tips Related to Employee Characteristics

THESE FIVE TIPS (32–36) ARE CRITICAL TO THE SUCCESS OF your humor. The size of your audience, and its composition in terms of gender, age, ethnicity, and mood can have a profound effect on their understanding of your humor and their willingness to laugh. Although you probably can't change those characteristics, you may be able to select or modify your humor material to ensure a reasonable level of success. Consider each of these factors carefully in planning your humor.

Super Size Your Audience

Guess what? You need an audience for your humor. A BIG audience. Employees should be lining up in droves to attend your meetings or speeches. The same thing should be happening for your workshops. Employees should be pounding on the doors to get in. However, in contrast, a seminar with five brilliant managers is not the best kick-off for testing humor material. The larger the audience or your workshop size, the greater the chance that there will be busloads of "laughers" scattered throughout the audience infecting the "nonlaughers" who otherwise might not respond.

Laughter is contagious. You want to contaminate as many people as possible. This contagion, unfortunately, reaches a point of diminishing returns after the first 1,000 persons. Remember, your audience wants to laugh. It's just waiting for you to say something hilarious.

In the real world, group sizes of 30–100 should be adequate to hone your skills. The point is that the next time you are given the opportunity to present to a large group of employees, whether you know the content or not (kidding), grab that opportunity by the throat and say: "Absolutely!"

Response to your humor will typically be very different in a tiny meeting or seminar of say, 5–10, compared to a similar group of several hundred. The unique group dynamics of the small group come into play. The employees' reactions to your humor tend to be based on the particular idiosyncratic personality combination of employees and your rapport with them. In general, this is not a fair test of your material. You need to be selective with small groups and, in some cases, you might want to modify the humor or the delivery.

If your humor doesn't work in a small group situation, don't discard it and don't be discouraged. The same material may be successful with another small group or a larger group. It would not be unusual for good humor material to totally bomb in a small meeting, but be received with thunderous laughter or applause at a meeting of 100 or more employees. Group size alone is a major determinant of the success of your humor.

TIP 33

Recruit Women into Your Audience

Females are the laughers; males are the jokesters. Women, in general, also tend to laugh at "clean," nonoffensive material, whereas many men prefer "dirty," raunchy, blue, or just plain stupid material that is inappropriate in the workplace. Of course, there are men and women who are exactly the reverse of these descriptions. So, if you use nonoffensive humor in your speeches, you can expect a greater positive response from women than from men.

The bottom line: You need people who will laugh at your humor. Women and girls laugh more than men and boys also because they're socialized differently. Laughter is the physical manifestation of an emotion. Males are socialized to be reserved, inhibited, stodgy, and downright anal about releasing or showing their emotions, including laughter. Some guys are simply as boring and expressive as milquetoast. The one exception to this generalization is at Super Bowl or other football parties. At parties every rule can be violated. The testosterone dripping off the walls brings out behaviors in men you probably won't see the rest of the year.

There are, of course, exceptions to these claims. Furthermore, laughter can also serve as a release valve for anxiety, stress, tension, nervousness, frustration, anger, and kleptomania. Whoever possesses those symptoms in your audience may also laugh more freely than other, better adjusted folks.

All of this boils down to the following rule of thumb: *A humor-friendly audience that will facilitate your success with humor should include at least 50% females.* The higher the percentage, the better your chances of laughter for the vast array of humor techniques you might want to attempt. Had it not been for the 90% female class composition in my courses over the last 19 years of my teaching, you probably would not be reading this page right now. It could not have been a more supportive environment for all the humor ideas I tested. However, despite that class composition, I still bombed regularly for other reasons, which I hope you will avoid.

So how are you supposed to apply this tip? Unless you have input into determining the gender composition of meetings and workshops, there's not a lot you can do. Most groups are assembled according to other criteria, such as expertise, project characteristics, and interpersonal skills. There may be numerous other factors that contribute to selection of employees. For training, people self-select themselves into workshops, or they are recommended by their bosses. Clearly, despite its importance to the success of your humor, you can't really manipulate your audience's gender in most situations. Just pray you get a reasonable percentage and try to be sensitive to that factor in the humor you choose.

TIP 34.

Gear Your Humor Toward the Majority Age in Your Audience

Employees in most organizations now seem to span multiple generations, from Veterans to the (Inter)Net Generation. Occasionally, employees enrolled in particular workshops may be more homogeneous, although there are exceptions. The point here is that different generations respond differently to most types of humor material. Age is one key factor that explains those differences.

You cannot alter the age composition of a group any more than you can change the gender distribution. In this case, what is critical to the success of your humor is your *sensitivity to the majority age and the distribution of other generations in your audience.* Although you may have a few younger and/or older employees than the majority age range in any given group, choose your humor content for the majority. For example, jokes about the difficulty of using the latest technology may be well-received by Boomers, but not by Net Geners. Humor about dating relationships may work with younger employees, whereas the Gen Xer and Boomer crowd would relate to humor about marriage, divorce, and parenting.

Up-close-and-personal experience: In general, among the 170 courses and 6,000 students I taught over my 30 years at Johns Hopkins, the youngest "20-something" students in my undergraduate classes have been the most receptive to every type of humor I have attempted, including stand-up jokes, anecdotes, multiple-choice jokes, top-10 lists, cartoons, TV, Broadway and movie parodies, and demonstrations with music. They tend to go with the flow, exhibiting a playful attitude and a willingness to have "fun" in class. They have a party mentality.

The older students in my master's classes became increasingly responsive to all forms of my humor over the last five years of my teaching. However, the older students in my doctoral classes have been less responsive to prepared humor material, but more receptive to spontaneous humor. They are more conservative, serious, and thesis obsessed, as well they should be, and they tend to be less flexible and willing to engage in "fun" activities. Class size differences among the class levels also had an impact on the students' reactions to humor. The undergraduate classes ranged from 50 to 125 students; master's classes from 20 to 40; and doctoral classes from 5 to 10.

You may also experience this variation in response to your humor. Until you've experimented with different humor material appropriate to the range of generations in your audiences, you won't have a feel for the age issue. It's critical. The bottom line: If the majority age group in your audience can't relate to, connect with, or understand your humor, pack it in. It's over. Rethink your humor and test it out informally with people in the target age group before using it in a formal speech.

TIP 35.

Use Humor Appropriate for Diverse Employees

Most of the humor material we see everywhere is culture specific. If an alien from the planet Snickers® visited us and watched our sitcoms or attended my workshops, it probably wouldn't laugh very much. That's because aliens don't have a sense of humor. WROONG! I'm told they have a terrific sense of humor; they just don't understand our culture. And they're not the only ones.

That's also the case for employees who come from different countries or cultures. Diversity in the workplace has taken on new dimensions. The cultural backgrounds of today's employees may indicate an appreciation of different forms of humor, and they may react to those forms differently. Unless you're immersed in the majority culture, it would be difficult to truly understand an Adam Sandler movie or to appreciate Chris Rock. Except for several TV sitcoms we have stolen or adapted from the Brit's originals (broadcast on PBS or BRAVO), most of the humor on TV and in the movies is verrry American.

How does this fact affect the humor you use in your workplace? First, you should be sensitive to the cultural backgrounds and diversity of all employees. Learn about them. Embrace the richness that their cultures can offer. Second, you should raise that sensitivity level to consider the forms and content of the humor you present. Sit down and chat with employees from other cultures face to face and ask them about the types of humor they like. What would be appropriate and inappropriate? Ask them about laughter in their culture. Are there restrictions?

I have discovered through presentations and individual chats that the *form of the humor,* such as multiple-choice joke, top 10, cartoon, or anecdote, is not as significant an issue as the *content* with people from Germany, Russia, Romania, Serbia, Hungary, Iran, Ukraine, and Poland. They are not familiar with American TV programs. My parodies of *CSI, X-Files, Masterpiece Theatre,* and *60 Minutes* were unappreciated for the humor, but understood for the concept.

Finally, employees from certain countries may not react to your humor as you expect. For example, there may be little or no laughter. In some cultures people suppress laughter; they do not feel free to let go emotionally. However, once they have been acculturated in the United States for a year or more, their laughter may be similar to that of the majority culture.

Culture-specific humor draws on material such as TV programs, commercials, infomercials, movies, Broadway musicals and plays, and American products and services advertised everywhere. Brand names of anything are inappropriate for employees from other countries.

In contrast, *culture-free humor* must be based on universal, generic topics that are not specific to any culture, country, or ethnic group. Here are a few examples:

- ✦ Relationships
  - Marriage (Be careful!)
  - Dating
  - Parenting
  - Living with teenagers
  - Manager-employee

- ✦ Music
  - Songs by internationally known artists
  - Mega-hit movies (e.g., *The Lord of the Rings, Star Wars, Rocky, Titanic*)
  - Musicals on international tours

- ✦ Miscellaneous
  - Pets

- Airlines (Be careful!)
- Coffee/tea
- Food
- Being young
- Getting old

The success of your humor with these employees hinges on how carefully you select or write material that is universal. I strongly caution you to avoid the trite, but, more importantly, inappropriate topics of sex, male and female bashing, and spousal put-downs, as well as attacks on politicians and internationally known celebrities. Although these relatively culture-free topics often constitute the heart of many stand-up comedians' monologues, they are out-of-bounds offensive material for any group of employees in a workplace setting.

Finally, avoid American jargon, slang, street language, and idioms in your humor that may be uninterpretable or misinterpreted (and possibly offensive). That type of language has become so pervasive in our culture that sometimes it's hard to discern the real meaning of the message. Sometimes even I cannot understand the jargon of Net Geners. I have purposely used idioms throughout these tips to set an informal tone, but I don't have a clue what they mean.

Up-close-and-personal experience: The preceding advice is derived not only from my classroom experiences, but from my presentations on humor to international audiences of professors and students. The absolutely scariest experience in my career as a humorist occurred in 2001 when I presented a keynote/plenary address on "Humor in Teaching" to 650 medical school professors from 60 countries at a European medical education conference at Humbolt University Medical School in Berlin. I was terrified. The joke examples, music, parodies, and demonstrations were pruned down to only the thoroughly tested material that I guessed everyone on earth would understand. I hit on 90%, missed on 10%. Part of my "miss" was *Jeopardy!*, which has a TV version in nearly every country in Europe. Yet, it fell flat. Go figure.

Other keynotes and workshops in Sweden, Norway, The Netherlands, Portugal, Italy, Germany, Serbia, United Arab Emirates, Czech Republic, and Scotland have met with similar success. When you use humor in other countries as a consultant or presenter at an international conference, ask the hosts about the content you plan on presenting. Be very selective in your choice of material. As I noted previously, when in doubt, leave it out.

TIP 36.

Be Sensitive to the Moods of Your Employees

Are you in touch with your employees' feelings and moods? (*CAU-TION*: This is the touchy-feely tip you have dreaded. If you survive this, you'll be okay.) If you're not in touch with your employees, talk to them. Find out what's going on in their lives. When you present humor, it must be appropriate to the affect in the room. *For each single piece of humor you have prepared for a speech, take two alternatives with you.* I always have three different "jokes" prepared. They may consist of a top 10, a multiple-choice joke, and an anecdote. Depending on the mood in the room, I may not go with my first-choice top 10. The content of the multiple-choice joke may seem more appropriate. Or, sometimes, the affect may say: "I'm not in the mood. Skip the humor today. If you tell a joke, you may regret it."

This strategy is applicable to all audiences, not just employees. I may not decide which joke to use until the moment I get to that point in my speech. I have a pool of material at my disposal. I also consider the audience's responses to earlier jokes. Based on those responses, I may select different material as the speech continues. This joke editing throughout a speech can be done inconspicuously with index cards at a lectern, but conspicuously by skipping slides in PowerPoint®. Your audience should not know you are picking out jokes at the last moment. In PowerPoint® I cover my tracks by saying: "In the interest of time, I have to skip over this material." I'm whizzing through the slides as I say that, so no one can see what was on those slides. Try to maintain a seamless flow while altering humor material as you proceed.

The bottom line is: BE FLEXIBLE. Be sensitive to your employees' feelings and responses to you at the beginning of your speech and choose the most appropriate humor from your pool or, maybe, none at all. If the audience is very quiet, something's probably wrong. If time permits before the meeting has begun, ask a few employees what's going on. This may not be the time for any opening joke.

The consequence of walking into a meeting with "canned humor" and just firing away, regardless of your employees' mood, can be "bombs away"—dead silence! Just as with the delivery of your humor, timing is critical. In this case, it's the timing of the humor itself.

When employees are noisy and rambunctious at the beginning of a meeting or workshop, their behavior may be the green light for your humor. They're ready to respond. That's the right time to blast off with whatever you have planned.

Summary

Let's review the five tips related to employee characteristics that significantly affect the success of humor:

32. Super Size Your Audience
33. Recruit Women into Your Audience
34. Gear Your Humor Toward the Majority Age in Your Audience
35. Use Humor Appropriate for Diverse Employees
36. Be Sensitive to the Moods of Your Employees

6

Tips for Creating a "Fun" Environment

THIS FINAL CHAPTER CONTAINS NINE TIPS (37–45) THAT CAN create an emotional atmosphere and physical environment conducive to a "fun" workplace. Tip 38 is probably the most important determinant of successful humor. The room atmosphere must be safe and playful, yet professional, to foster humor. There are also physical room configurations and factors that can affect the responsiveness of employees to your humor efforts. All of these tips can make a difference in your success.

Create a Safe Environment for Humor

Laughter is an emotional release. Employees must feel free to let their guard down to laugh. If they're tense, stressed, anal, or all of the preceding, you will not hear laughs; instead, you will get looks, straaange ones.

A safe environment for humor depends on the types of humor permissible at the coffee pot, in the hallways, in the boardroom, and in the meeting rooms. For example, if employees can expect put-downs, sarcasm, ridicule, or other forms that may be offensive, they may feel threatened or tense about being the next potential target or victim of some barb by you or another employee (see chapter 1).

Safety hinges on knowing the rules of your humor game—what's appropriate and inappropriate. That starts at the top of the organization. Humor should be a core value. As noted in chapter 1, your business's standards for humor should be communicated early and clearly, perhaps at the beginning of the year. Make sure everyone knows the rules and the consequences for breaking them. Creating a safe, nonthreatening, relaxed atmosphere in your workplace is absolutely essential for the humor to be well-received by your employees. Ultimately, this can lead to a "fun" work environment.

TIP 38

Create a Playful, but Professional, Room Atmosphere

This is my nomination for the *number one reason why good humor material fails in the meeting room.* Unless the atmosphere is conducive to laughter, the humor will bomb.

Consider this scenario:

1. Manager presents a PowerPoint® speech from notes while standing at the lectern.
2. Room atmosphere is formal and serious.
3. During the course of the speech, the manager tells a joke or makes a "humorous" comment and there is no laughter or any audible response. Total silence.

As extreme as this might appear, it is a real situation in many meetings. What happened? Why didn't the audience respond? Probably because either they didn't recognize the joke, or they didn't feel safe enough to laugh or express an emotional reaction.

Laughter occurs in casual and relaxed environments where people feel safe and free to be uninhibited. Unfortunately, virtually all business is SERIOUS! We're trained to be serious. That's dignified and professional. Employees are conditioned from the time they're fetuses to think that productivity in business is serious business. Play is what you do in the bar, lounge, or a friend's house. The workplace atmosphere is supposed to be different from what happens outside. Right? Unless employees are conditioned otherwise in your business, they will not be able to identify a joke, even when it hits them smack in the kidney. Ouuuch! A playful state of mind is a necessary, but not sufficient, precondition for humor appreciation and laughter.

The character of the managers and other employees and the room atmosphere must be a mixture of *serious* AND *playful* in order for humor to succeed. The tone and mood you set will transfer to your employees. They need to know when it's appropriate (or okay) to fool around or laugh and when serious business needs to be accomplished. The obvious question is: Where's the rest of this paragraph? Oops. Got it. How does a manager or trainer create this atmosphere?

First, anything you do that deviates from your normally serious demeanor will help. But you need to go beyond that. It's all related to your rapport or connection with your colleagues and employees. Your words and actions inside and outside the room must convey playfulness. Here are four suggestions:

1. ***Outside of the room***, schmooze with your employees. When you see them at the coffee pot, in the hallways, snack bar, cafeteria, celebration, or holiday gathering, joke around or tease them, etc. You know what I mean. Let them expect you to be nonserious. Remember, this is nonoffensive banter.

2. ***In your office***, before a serious meeting, joke with the employee if the time seems appropriate. The humor may help the person relax. However, be sensitive to the person's mood and the context of the meeting before joking. The time and place must be right.

3. ***Before work begins***, as people are settling in with their coats, briefcases, backpacks, snowshoes, and other gear, kid around with them. I usually say something like: "How are you? How's the family?" (which they don't expect) "Long time no see!" "Thanks for dropping by today." Tease them about the bags they're carrying, the breakfast food they're eating, the color of their ski caps, and so on. This sets a tone and a

rapport that will carry through the rest of the day. This pre-work banter expresses your personal interest in your colleagues and a lightheartedness that can take the formal, serious sting out of the work that follows.

4. ***At the beginning of a meeting, speech, or workshop,*** open with a joking question about some current event issue at work or outside work, or a question everyone can answer. Try a cartoon, bumper sticker, anecdote, humorous hand-out, or stand-up joke. This opening says to your employees: "Let's unwind and play for a minute before moving into the serious content." It can serve as a release valve for you and your employees as well as a hook to grab their attention before the "serious stuff." My openings usually consume 30 seconds to 1.5 minutes. The longest has been 3 minutes. After your opening, inject humorous comments throughout the meeting or workshop, but never put-downs of anyone.

Given the relationships created by your previous actions, *your employees should now be your greatest supporters. They're your allies; your best friends.* They will feel free to react to any humor you attempt. They're rooting for you. They want you to succeed. You've paved the way to an environment ripe for laughter.

Although your employees' reactions may not always be laughter, perhaps sometimes only a smile, they will recognize your effort and respond in some positive way. Now you just need to prepare funny material or deliver a witty response to someone's question to elicit full-blown laughter. For example, if an employee asks several questions during a meeting, you could say: "That question hit the bull's-eye again. You're on fire. Can I have a sip of whatever you're drinking?"

TIP 39

Get Close to Your Employees, but Not Too Close

Physical proximity can affect your relationship with your audience and, ultimately, the success of your humor. Closeness engenders a connection of supportiveness and empathy; distance minimizes any positive affective connection.

Comedy clubs are intimate. The stage is small and very close to the audience. When Jay Leno succeeded Johnny Carson on the *Tonight Show,* he had an extension built from the original stage, which put him on the same level and close to the audience. It rolls out from under the stage; hence, the name *tongue.* When he comes out every night, the first thing he does is step down onto the tongue and shake hands with as many people as he can. This closeness and the physical contact establish an emotional connection with his audience from the get-go. He is right in their faces. They are already in his corner, and he hasn't even told a joke yet.

You need to create this type of comedy club connection with your employees, whether in the boardroom, general meeting room, or auditorium. First, get a tongue. Wait. You probably don't need one. It's simple: *Just walk out into your audience as you are telling a joke or anecdote.* It can be a stand-up type joke or a format projected in PowerPoint® where each line in a multiple-choice item or top 10 flies in on cue.

Why is this physical connection so important? Because humor stimulates emotional (mirth) and physical (laughter) responses. Standing close to your employees as you move around the room elicits an emotional connection. Humor builds on this positive affect. (*Alternatively:* A negative, intimidating demeanor can scare the audience to death, or worse.) People are more prone to laugh at a joke told by a speaker with whom they have a warm, emotional connection than by one who is cold and distant. The speaker who stands at a lectern a mile away from his or her audience creates a physical distance and barrier (the lectern), which is typically formal and cold. One does not have to be formal, cold, and distant to be professional. The physical open space between a speaker and his or her lectern and the audience is called a "comedy moat." That moat fosters an emotional separation from your employees that is not conducive to laughter.

Eliminate that moat, and mingle with your employees. The closeness you create physically will make a difference in their response to everything you do in your speeches, especially the humor. As you walk around the audience, your proximity alone may keep their attention and have them sitting on the edges of their seats in anticipation that you might single them out for a question or other form of input. That's always intimidating.

 **TIP 40**

Establish Eyeball-to-Eyeball Contact

WARNING:

This page talks about—yup, you guessed it—eyeballs. DO NOT read these sentences, especially the quotes, without first putting on safety goggles. Otherwise, the highly graphic interocular description may pop your eyeballs—sproiiing—out of their sockets so that they end up dangling from their optic fibers around your kneecaps. Beeee careful.

Building on the comedy club connection, make eye contact with as many employees as possible as you are telling a joke or anecdote. Your eyeballs create an electrical connection that is very personal.

You're sending the following message: "I really hope you laugh at this material, because I don't have a clue what I'm doing chairing this meeting."

Your employees are thinking: "You are such a loser. With your meager abilities and dangling eyeballs, it's surprising that you're moderately funny. Ha."

Eye contact facilitates the emotional connection that can increase the success of your humor. Stop for the two-second pause that refreshes your connection. That connection can increase the audience's memory of what you said.

TIP 41

Smush the Seats Together

What does the seating arrangement look like in your rooms? Theater-style with chairs lined up in rows? Classroom-style with long or circular tables and chairs? Chairs surrounding a large boardroom table? Random scatter of super-uncomfortable chairs? Cushions or pillows on the floor as in a Lamaze class?

Well, get rid of the furniture. Kidding. For this tip, you really don't need to hire an interior decorator. The goal is simply to have everyone sit as close together as possible without breathing each other's oxygen AND, if possible, to be able to see each other. *A close, intimate environment where people can see others laughing at the humor is the most conducive atmosphere for laughter.* As you already know, laughter is contagious. Being right next to someone who is laughing or watching others laugh can put employees who are teetering on the edge of hysteria over the top. I'm not sure why they're teetering, but they are pushed over the top because laughter is reflexive. It's like seeing someone yawn, which would be your worst nightmare in this case.

What physical structure can produce the best possible situation for laughter? Any of the seating arrangements I mentioned above can work as long as the chairs are smushed together. Further, try to arrange the chairs in a semi-circle facing the front of the room so employees can see one another. Straight rows of chairs are usually less effective. If your employees are sitting at round tables, that's fine. The large boardroom table also works because from any seat, a person can see three quarters of the group. Whatever rearrangement of chairs you can complete before a meeting or workshop starts will contribute to the success of your humor.

TIP 42

If the Room's Too Big, Tape Off Sections

All of your employees need to be in the smushed-together chairs. That will increase the probability that the "laughers" will infect the "marginal laughers" and, by some miracle, maybe even the "non-laughers." However, if your room is too large for the size of the meeting, for example, 10 managers and 50 seats (Like, who assigns the rooms anyway? What were they thinking?), usually the managers will fill the last row first and then scatter hither and yon. Most people are afraid to sit up front in any live meeting or workshop or church, synagogue, or mosque. Some would prefer to sit in hither; others in yon.

You have three options to get the employees to the front of the room and together: (1) ask them politely, at which point they will feign deafness and not budge, (2) order them forcefully and threaten them, at which point they will feign deafness and not budge, or (3) tape off the upper rows with yellow and black "Crime Scene" tape from *CSI*. If you opt for (3) and know you have employees who have a rap sheet or who possess criminal potential, you might want to reinforce (3) by saying: "If anyone moves or removes the tape, there WILL BE a crime scene. Don't even think about it." Now you can play some nice soft music to relax your employees until you're ready to begin. Maybe the "Who Are You?" theme from *CSI* or the "Doink, Doink!" from *Law & Order* will do the trick.

TIP 43

Schedule Your Meetings and Workshops in Late Morning

Yeah right! If you are so blessed as to have control over the meeting or workshop schedule, shoot for late morning. That time can produce the highest number of Laughs Per Minute (LPM).

When do most people NOT feel like laughing? The *worst times* are early morning and after lunch from 2–5 PM. At these times, except for those "early risers" who want to torment the rest of us, most employees aren't completely awake yet, or they want to go back to sleep. It is tough getting laughs at 8:30 on Monday, Tuesday, and Wednesday mornings, which is when my undergraduate biostatistics classes were scheduled for the last 19 years I taught.

The *best times* for laughter are late morning (10–12) and early evening. People are conditioned to be entertained in the evening; after all, that is prime time for TV sitcoms, movies, and the theater. Just make me laugh! However, after working all day, employees are looking forward to "Happy Hour!" outside the workplace.

By a process of elimination, that leaves late morning. Try scheduling some meetings and workshops within that time period. Notice whether the employees' level of responsiveness is different compared to other times. Gauge your scheduling to take advantage of their responsiveness, if possible. Their peak times also can increase their engagement and memory of your message.

TIP 44

Keep the Room Temperature Cool

Heat produces discomfort, sleepiness, sweat, and even riots, killings, and special effects. This is not the optimum condition for employees to laugh. Although there are certain gender and age combinations of employees who prefer either tropical room temperatures or frigid ones, I recommend that you keep your room thermostat on the cooler side. Employees who are alert or just borderline conscious tend to be more receptive to humor than those who are nodding out. Even if a few of your employees need to don ski apparel, they won't fall asleep and, if they do, their bodies will be better preserved. The evidence indicates that cryogenics works!

TIP 45

Eliminate All Distractions

When you're giving a speech as well as trying to be funny, your employees should be totally focused on YOU. However, that focus can be pulled away from you if the sun is streaming in the side windows and blinding the employees on the ends of rows; cell phones are playing "Beethoven's Fifth"; or some employees are crunching on Sugar Crispy Captain Crackling No-Fat Frosted Flakes. You don't need those distractions.

Try to eliminate the potential sources of distraction before the meeting or workshop begins. Distractions may not only decrease the employees' responsiveness to your humor, but they could even throw off your timing. Although unexpected disruptions can create spontaneous humor moments, they're still disconcerting during the delivery of prepared humor. You want as much control as possible over the employees' emotional mood and the physical room atmosphere to maximize the effectiveness of your humor.

Summary

Let's review the nine tips for creating an emotional and physical environment conducive to "fun" in your workplace:

37. Create a Safe Environment for Humor
38. Create a Playful, but Professional, Room Atmosphere
39. Get Close to Your Employees, but Not Too Close
40. Establish Eyeball-to-Eyeball Contact
41. Smush the Seats Together
42. If the Room's Too Big, Tape Off Sections
43. Schedule Your Meetings and Workshops in Late Morning
44. Keep the Room Temperature Cool
45. Eliminate All Distractions

7

Creating TV, Movie, and Broadway Parodies

THE PARODY IS ONE OF THE HIGHEST FORMS OF HUMOR. It can be used in the workplace to provide blockbuster openings for meetings and workshops, to introduce agenda items or topics for discussion, to create team-building exercises, to furnish a humor spin for a demonstration or skit with employees, or to give collaborative employee projects a unique perspective. This chapter presents step-by-step procedures to make those parodies a reality. These procedures are based on 10 years of experience and the research on the effectiveness of the parody as a communications tool. The parody also provides a direct link with the characteristics and culture of the Net Generation and draws on their multiple intelligences. It is one of the most powerful humor techniques you can use.

Definition of Parody with Examples

Let's begin with the definition of parody. Consider the following:

- ◆ *a composition that imitates somebody's style in a humorous way*
- ◆ *make a spoof of or make fun of*
- ◆ *humorous or satirical mimicry*
  (http://wordnet.princeton.edu/perl/webwn)

I think the most appropriate definition is

- ◆ *a work, often humorous, that imitates another work, usually serious*
  (http://ww2.aps.edu/users/apsedumain/CurriculumInstruction/
  glossary.htm)

The object or target of the parody can be a specific

1. person (style, ideas, or work)
2. place
3. event
4. work of art, literature, or performing arts (music, theater, TV, or other media)

In other words, we begin with a serious TV program, such as *CSI, Law & Order,* or *House;* a serious action movie, like *Mission: Impossible, Bourne Ultimatum,* or *Star Wars;* or a serious musical, such as *Chicago, The Phantom of the Opera,* or *Les Misérables.* The parody can then twist the seriousness of these works or their characters into something humorous.

People watch parodies regularly on TV, YouTube, and in the movies. You should make every effort to involve employees in the planning and execution of these parody productions. The possibilities are limited only by your imagination and creativity. You are the writer, director, choreographer, and scenic, lighting, sound, and costume designer. It's all in the preparation. If you survey your employees on what they watch, the results can suggest several possible parodies. You can also get ideas from the following lists. Most of the TV parodies appear on *Comedy Central* and the movies have become cult classics:

TV Programs	Movies	Broadway Musicals
The Daily Show	Scary Movie 1–4	The Producers
Colbert Report	Austin Powers	Young Frankenstein
Reno 911!	Airplane!	Spamalot
MAD TV	Scream I–IV	Avenue Q
SNL	Fatal Instinct	Forbidden Broadway
Chappelle's Show	Not Another Teen Movie	
Mind of Mensia	Young Frankenstein	
South Park	The Producers	
Scrubs	Blazing Saddles	
	Monty Python and the Holy Grail	

Is there any theoretical or research evidence to support the use of parodies in training? Absolutely!

A parody:

1. Provides a HOOK! (a.k.a. immediate engagement)
2. Draws on four to six multiple intelligences, including
   a. verbal or quantitative
   b. visual/spatial
   c. bodily/kinesthetic
   d. musical/rhythmic
   e. interpersonal
   f. intrapersonal
3. Uses music which creates
   a. mood
   b. humor

    c. visual imagery

    d. personal connection

4. Promotes demonstrations to

    a. grab employees' attention and focus

    b. increase interest in topic

    c. reduce anxiety and stress

    d. make topic/training/ learning fun

    e. facilitate understanding of topic

    f. increase memory of topic

    g. improve learning of content

Six Steps to Creating a Parody

1. *Determine the pool of possible TV programs, movies, or Broadway shows to parody.*

Consider the following sources for parody material:

- ◆ *TV programs* based on Nielsen Media Research survey results for adults
- ◆ *Movies* based on cult classics, Oscar winners, and most recent and popular flicks
- ◆ *Musical comedies* performed recently, locally and on Broadway
- ◆ Results of an informal student survey of what your employees watch
- ◆ Results of a formal survey of their preferences

Let's chat about the surveys for a moment. As an informal survey, just ask a sample of employees their preferences. You should talk to them at every opportunity to find out their favorite TV programs, movies, and Broadway shows. What are they watching? Usually, they love to tell you what TV programs to watch or what movies to see.

Further, you should conduct a formal survey of employees either online or manually during a large meeting where most people will be present at an appropriate time during the year. The information gleaned from that survey can furnish a wealth of information for potential parodies. Follow the procedures described in Tip 5. The focus questions in this survey should deal with

- *3 favorite TV programs*
- *3 favorite movies* seen during the past 3–6 months
- *3 favorite Broadway shows*
- *favorite commercials* or *YouTube video clips*

Now you can compute a frequency distribution of the top-10 TV programs the employees are watching. First, simply count, for example, how many people chose *CSI*, then repeat for *Deal or No Deal*, then repeat for every other program written on a card. Second, rank the programs by those numbers from high to low. Finally, cut off the list at the 10th program to identify the top 10.

A distribution should then be computed for each of the other three card sides. Those distributions will yield four top-10 lists that provide a pool of shows from which parodies can be created for the entire year. From these sources, you can develop TV, movie, Broadway show, and commercial parodies with which most of the employees are familiar. These parodies can be presented at meetings and workshops. They can dramatize a point related to a specific learning outcome in workshops and seminars.

If audience members don't know the original show, then the parody will be meaningless. Since we're using only the "most frequent," not everyone will get every parody. But it's still possible to have a very high hit rate if you choose the blockbusters that most people recognize. You have more than 40 different shows from which to select the biggies. This is your most accurate pool of material for parodies.

2. *Choose a TV program, movie, or Broadway show to parody.*

Here are a few shows to think about when deciding what to parody:

TV Programs	Movies	Broadway Musical
CSI	Star Wars	The Odd Couple
Grey's Anatomy	Titanic	Chicago
Deal or No Deal	Mission: Impossible	The Phantom of the Opera
Jeopardy!	Lord of the Rings	Les Misérables
American Idol	Psycho	Spamalot
Law & Order	Jaws	Rent
24	Scary Movie	The Producers
The Daily Show	Rocky	Beauty & the Beast
Sesame Street	Dreamgirls	The Lion King
Masterpiece Theatre		Spring Awakening

We're going to use *CSI* as an example to build a parody. It's been in the Nielsen top 10 consistently over the past several years, and even if you've never watched it, you probably have enough information from the trailers to create a parody.

3. *Determine the topic or content for which you want to create a parody.*

- ✦ Topics
  - —name of topic
  - —letter or number that has significance related to the topic
- ✦ Basic concepts/principles/processes
  - —relationships between people or things
  - —tools of the trade or activity
  - —comparison and contrast for any topic
- ✦ Complex or technical topics

Our topic is "workplace issues."

4. ***Transform the title of the program, movie, show, character, or song.***

Use a rhyming dictionary to assist in generating a play on title words.

What do workplace issues have to do with *CSI*? Nothing! Nada! Zippo! The challenge is to change the *CSI* title into something related to workplace issues. Let's play with the initials, *CSI*. Instead of Crime Scene Investigation, what three words could you use that relate to work issues that begin with *C S* and *I*?

Let's do this one letter at a time—brainstorm with me.

What are some C words? career, cope, complain, corporate, customer, client, cooperative, collaborative, chairs, computers, concentration, create, content

What about words for the letter S? simulation, secondary, script, success, stress, staff, schedule, service

What about I? improvise, iPod, intentional, incite, intelligence, interest, imagination, inspire, increase, improve

Now, try different word combinations for *CSI*

CSI: *Create Stress Intentionally*
 Customer Success Increases
 Career Service Inspires
 Corporate Success Improves
 Complaining Staff Increases

You now have several examples of a play on words from the TV hit *CSI*.

5. ***Write, direct, choreograph, and stage the parody.***

> ◆ Think about every element that can be exaggerated to the most ridiculous extreme possible.

✦ Determine the visual image you want to create using the following (visualization):
  — *Props*
  — *Costumes*
  — *Lighting*
  — *Set (chairs, tables, etc.)*
  — *Background*
  — *Movement*
✦ Determine music and equipment you will need (instrument or CD player/PowerPoint®).
✦ Determine the number of employee participants:
  — *Prepare participants in advance*
  — *Consider understudies*

Let's now apply this to our *CSI* parody: *What props, costumes, and lighting are typical of CSI?*

Even in the trailers, we always see flashlights, latex gloves, scenes in the dark with rain, crime scene tape, and so on.

How can we exaggerate those key elements?

Props	Costume	Lighting
flashlights	*surgical gloves*	*opening blackout*
headlights	*crime scene tape sash*	
book on stress management		

Now, what about the setting, background, and movement?

Set	Background	Movement
Darken classroom	*CSI slide*	*Run through room*

Finally, what about the music and cast of participants?

Music	Participants
CSI theme	*Trainer only*

Add animation and music to slide.

6. *Practice the Parody.*
   - ◆ Entrance and exit—Will you have a special entrance and exit or just begin while you're standing in front of the class?
   - ◆ Blackouts and lighting—Who will handle the lighting?
   - ◆ Start and stop music—Who will control remote for slides and music?
   - ◆ Access to props—Where are you going to hide the props and then grab them quickly when you need them?
   - ◆ Costume change—What costume change is necessary and where are you going to do it?
   - ◆ Employee rehearsal—You need to rehearse, but so do the employee participants.

What would be involved in practicing the *CSI* parody? Let's go through a rehearsal:

1. Begin by standing in front of the room and introducing the topic: "Today we're going to try out a technique for managing stress."
2. Nod your head to the person at the light switch, giving the signal to turn out all lights. The signal for turning them back on is "When the music stops."
3. Drop down under the table in front of the room, which contains all of the props. They are covered by a canvas bag. Turn on a small flashlight so you can see what you're doing. First, put the crime scene tape sash over your head. Second, put on the latex surgical gloves. Third, put on the headlight and turn it on. Finally, turn on the two small Maglite® headlights, one in each hand.
4. Now stand up and put down the right flashlight to click the remote from the black slide on the screen to the *CSI* green slide with the theme music.

5. Drop the remote on the table as the music begins, pick up the small flashlight, and start racing around the room, pointing the flashlights in the employees' hair and mouths, behind an employee's chair, then to the back of the room where you have hidden a book on stress management. Listening to the music carefully, run to the front of the room so that you will end as the music is ending; wave the book over your head. The whole running around routine goes very quickly, because the song "Who Are You?" lasts only 33 seconds, the typical length of most TV themes.

6. The whole parody takes a little more than a minute. When the music stops, an employee turns the lights back on.

7. Hold up the book and start talking about the topic as you take off the gloves, sash, and headlight, and turn off all of the flashlights. This is a really great intro for a personal issue such as stress. This parody can relax an uptight, anxious audience.

7. *Performance debut.*

NOW, IT'S *YOUR* TURN . . .

Set up five-person parody production teams of employees. They form collaborative learning groups. There are five roles in each production team:

1. *Director:* guides everyone to focus on an idea that creates the parody with/without script

2. *Designer:* creates scenery, costumes, props, lighting, sound, music, sound effects, and/or videos

3. *Technician:* determines technical equipment, tools, and resources to execute parody

4. *Stage Manager:* manages the time, location, and logistics

5. *Actor(s):* performs parody

Summary

Here again are the six major steps for creating a parody:

1. Determine the pool of possible TV programs, movies, and Broadway shows to parody.
2. Choose a TV program, movie, or Broadway show to parody.
3. Determine the topic or content for which you want to create a parody.
4. Transform the title of the program, movie, show, character, or song.
5. Write, direct, choreograph, and stage the parody.
6. Practice the parody until you feel ready for your meeting or workshop debut.

QUICK ORDER FORM
(copy this form)

Fax orders: 1-888-401-8089. Send a copy of this form.

Telephone orders: 1-410-730-9339. Have your credit card ready.

Email orders: rberk@son.jhmi.edu

Postal orders: Coventry Press
10971 Swansfield Rd.
Columbia, MD 21044

Please send _____ copies (fewer than 15) of *Top Secret Tips for Successful Humor in the Workplace* at $16.95 each

Sales tax: Please add 6% for Maryland addresses.

Shipping cost: $6.95 for first copy, $3.00 for each additional copy

Checks payable to: Coventry Press

Quantity discounts: See next page or www.coventrypress.com

SEND BOOK(S) TO:

Name: _____

Address: _____

City: _____ **State:** _____ **Zip:** _____

Phone: _____ **Email:** _____

Credit card: __VISA __MasterCard **Exp. Date:** _____

Card Number: _____

CSC (3-digit no.) _____ **Name on card:** _____

Signature: _____ **Date:** _____

SEND ME FREE INFORMATION ON THE FOLLOWING:

_____ Speaking   ____Consulting   ____Other Books & Products

QUANTITY DISCOUNTS

IF YOU HAVE BOOKED RON BERK TO SPEAK AT YOUR
INSTITUTION, YOU ARE ENTITLED TO RECEIVE SPECIAL
DISCOUNTED PRICES ON:

Top Secret Tips for Successful Humor in the Workplace (2009)

(List price = $16.95)   (*Note:* Shipping costs extra.)

QUANTITY	COST PER BOOK	TOTAL
15–29	$15.00	$225 +
30–59	$14.00	$420 +
60–99	$13.00	$780 +
100–299	$12.00	$1200 +
300 +	$10.00	$3000 +

SIX Reasons to Pre-Order Books

1. *INCREASE ATTENDANCE* by advertising that everyone (or the first _____ who register) will receive a FREE book. If conference fee is several hundred dollars and at least 100 people attend, a $10 or $12 add-on is insignificant.
2. *REWARD EMPLOYEES or FACULTY* for something special they did or for outstanding performance.
3. *USE AS DOOR PRIZES* and benefit from the lower prices.
4. *ANNOUNCE A BOOK SIGNING* in advance to increase attendance and give people a lower rate.
5. *RECEIVE THE DISCOUNTED PRICE,* which is lower than the normal book signing discount.
6. *RAISE MONEY FOR YOUR INSTITUTION* by buying books at the discounted price and selling them at the event for a slight mark-up.

I am interested in ordering _____ (Qty.) copies of
Top Secret Tips for Successful Humor in the Workplace

Name (print or type) _____

Signature _____

Fax order: 1-888-410-8089 OR Call: 1-410-730-9339

LaVergne, TN USA
18 August 2010
193804LV00003B/12/P